# PAGAN
# WAYS

# Is Paganism Right for You?

*Pagan Ways* is an introductory guide to the most common elements of modern Paganism. Learn how to create and perform your own rituals. Discover a spiritual path that celebrates the seasons and honors the world in which we live. Bring a sense of renewal into your life by participating in the changing of the seasons and the ever-turning wheel of the year. Experience a fulfilling way of life that is as valid today as it was when people worked and lived in close connection to the Earth and the elements.

Across the world, there is a longing for the Earth-centered spirituality of our ancestors. Many feel the need for the return of the guiding wisdom and gentle magick of the Old Religion. *Pagan Ways* is your first step toward finding your own spiritual truth through the beauty and power of the natural world.

## About the Author

Gwydion O'Hara is dedicated to the research, study, and practice of the ancient folk ways that survive today. For over twenty years, he has studied the practices of the people of the land, wherever and however they present themselves. It is this calling that has led him to write this book, as well as his previous offerings *Sun Lore* and *Moon Lore*.

He has traveled across the United States and Canada in the pursuit of his studies in herbology, mythology, folklore, tarot, the Pagan craft, and folk magic. Along the way, he has met, taught, and learned from many others who share his love of the old ways.

## To Write to the Author

If you wish to contact the author or would like more information about this book, please write to the author in care of Llewellyn Worldwide, and we will forward your request. Both the author and publisher appreciate hearing from you and welcome your comments. Llewellyn Worldwide cannot guarantee a reply to all letters, but all will be forwarded. Please write to:

Gwydion O'Hara
℅ Llewellyn Worldwide
P.O. Box 64383, Dept. K341-7
St. Paul, MN 55164-0383, U.S.A.

Please enclose a self-addressed, stamped envelope or $1.00 to cover costs. If outside the U.S.A., enclose an international postal reply coupon.

# PAGAN

# WAYS

*Finding Your Spirituality in Nature*

# Gwydion O'Hara

1998
Llewellyn Publications
St. Paul, MN 55164-0383 U.S.A.

**FIRST EDITION**
Second Printing, 1998

Cover design: Lisa Novak
Editing and book design: Ken Schubert
Interior illustrations: Ric Allendorf

**Library of Congress Cataloging-in-Publication Data**
O'Hara, Gwydion.
    Pagan Ways : finding your spirituality in nature / Gwydion O'Hara
    — 1st. ed.
        p.    cm.
    Includes bibliographical references.
    ISBN 1-56718-341-7   (pbk. )
    1. Neopaganism.  2. Spiritual life.
    3. Nature—Religious aspects.
I.  Title.
BF1566.O33   1997
299—dc21                                         97-22994
                                                      CIP

Printed in the U.S.A.

Llewellyn Publications
A Division of Llewellyn Worldwide, Ltd.
P.O. Box 64383
St. Paul, MN 55164-0383, U.S.A.

*To those who would teach—*
*may they never cease to learn.*

# Contents

## Contents

# Author's Note

There are many terms that are used throughout the body of this volume that are almost interchangeable. These arise from the names by which Pagans have been known throughout history, as well as the terms by which they recognize themselves, some from modern times, some from long ago. For this reason, a glossary has been included in the back of this volume to assist the reader in wading through the verbiage.

It is important, however, to mention a few of the more commonly used terms up front, before the reader becomes overwhelmed by the many terms that are bandied (quite freely) about. The following list should suffice for a start:

*Craeft*: An archaic spelling of "craft" used to describe Pagan worship. The term takes its roots from the phrase "Craft of the Wise," a presumed meaning of Wicca (see below).

*Pagan*: Originally derived from the word *pagani*, meaning a dweller of the land, this name has come to mean a follower of one of the nature religions practiced in times past.

*Old Religion*: Paganism.

*Wicca:* A popular term in more recent times. This can indicate the practice of Pagan ways, the following of one of the newer expressions of nature religion, or the priesthood of the Pagans (the initiates). It is believed that this word arises from the Anglo-Saxon root *wicce*, which means "to know." Hence, Wicca is the Craft of the Wise.

*Witchcraft:* When Pagan worship was branded heresy, it became more popular to accuse the victim of witchcraft than of Paganism. Not so much by actual meaning, but by connotation, this seemed a far more grievous crime. Today, the priesthood of the Pagans often consider themselves "witches." It is often held as a badge of honor, deriving from the same root as Wicca, indicating wisdom.

# Acknowledgements

Without the care and close working relationship of many of the staff at Llewellyn Worldwide, this offering, as well as those before it, would have never found its way to the bookshelf.

Though they remain in the background to those who read the printed word, much of the glory of this volume belongs to them. With much gratitude, a thank you is due and highly deserved to my own "unsung heroes."

# Chapter One

## *Our Pagan Roots*

The beginnings of Paganism lie as far back as the dawn of humanity. Before the rise of civilization, the primitive tribes could watch the progression of the Sun and Moon across the sky, and the constant change of the seasons. In the summer months, they depended on the growth of the plant life of the earth to sustain their lives. In winter, the green earth fell barren and the flesh of the animals became a major food staple for the people.

Everywhere they looked, our ancestors saw the cycles of life within nature. It was readily apparent that their own lives were dependent on the continued march of the seasons. Without the rains, there would be no fresh water to drink, and the fields would burn up beneath the hot sun. Without the time of rest in winter, the fertile soil would be stripped of the nutrients that helped the plants to grow strong and the fruit to ripen on the boughs.

Everywhere they turned, people found the inescapable truth—that they were at the mercy of powerful and mysterious forces. And so they sought to gain the approval of the divine forces behind nature by giving them worship. In order to gain assurance that the trees would bear fruit when the summer sun was high, and that the hunt would be successful when snow covered the lands, they sought to appease the authors of these uncontrollable forces.

The plant life was thought to be the domain of the Goddess. It was seen how new life issued forth from the womb of a woman; so must it be in the natural order that a female deity caused the plant life to emerge from the womb of the earth.

The hunt was primarily the responsibility of the men of the tribe, since their more heavily muscled frame and speed of foot gave a better chance of success, and since the women needed to stay near the safety of home while they suckled the young. So it was the men that set out on the hunt, and reasoned that the deity who granted its success must also be a masculine figure.

In Ariege, France, archaeologists discovered a cave painting of a primitive figure adorned in the skins and horns of an animal, performing a ritual dance. This painting has been dated to the late Paleolithic period, or approximately 10,000 B.C., and is believed to be one of the earliest depictions of a man in a ritual observance.

Presumably, the stone age artisan believed that by adorning himself with the skins and horns of the animals he hunted, and by performing the proper rites, he could gain the favor of the God of the Hunt. The primitive hunters could then depend on the help of the God to ensure that their quest was bountiful, and by extension that their people would be well fed through the winter.

A Horned God, a God of the Hunt, has been a prominent figure throughout many cultures and has taken a visible role in the mythologies of many lands. In Asia, Greece, Rome, and the Celtic lands of Europe, the Horned God watched as civilizations rose and fell. Tribal rites in parts of Africa, in the islands of the Pacific Ocean, among the Arctic Eskimos, and among Native peoples of North and South America have included acts of reverence to a Horned God.

As agriculture grew, the need for hunting decreased. In many cultures, the Horned God became a fertility deity. One of the most widely recognized images of the Horned God in this aspect can be found in the vision of Pan, the goat-footed God of the Greeks. Pan is well remembered for his sexual appetite and proficiency.

Representatives of the female principle of nature have also enjoyed a long history of adoration, and have made their homes among the peoples of many different cultures throughout the world. In the earliest times, it was obvious to all that women had the miraculous ability to bear children. But without the light of knowledge and the hand of science to guide primitive understanding, it was not apparent that the male had any role in the creation of life. Birth was thought to be exclusively a female mystery. The Goddess, therefore, was regarded as a fertility deity, and worshiped as the creative force.

In times and cultures where hunting was the major source of food, the God of the Hunt was revered as a supreme deity, and religion and society took on a patriarchal slant. When it was the fruit of the land that became paramount to survival, it was the Goddess who reigned supreme, and society and religious expression took on a more matriarchal character. Yet, though supremacy swung back and forth between the male and female deities, seldom has one been revered to the exclusion of the other.

Even within cultures that held a pantheon of deities sacred, there were often two, a male and a female, who reigned above all. In Egypt, Isis and Osiris were often regarded as the supreme entities. The Greeks knew Zeus and Hera as the king and queen of the universe, father and mother of all the lesser Gods and Goddesses. The Saxons revered Woden and Freya, and the Welsh adored Arianrod and Gwydion as the greatest among the hero-gods.

Even after the rise of Christianity, the God and Goddess were freely worshiped. The Pagan religions were of the land and of the people. They were a part of each waking moment, and each act of nature reminded the Pagans of the God and Goddess that they adored. The new Christians were not likely to uproot the ways that the Pagan people had practiced through many generations. In fact, in the early days of Christianity, the new religion and its zealous practitioners were not taken very seriously at all. Well known are the tales of the Coliseum in Rome where the new Christians were regarded as little more than sport and dinner for lions.

In time, however, Christianity began to gain strength. By the year A.D. 312, it had become the official church of the decaying Roman empire, and dwelt side by side along with the Pagan practices of the common folk. Over time, the Christian fathers were very successful in winning over the sovereigns of Europe, and one land at a time, the new faith became the official religion.

Still, they had not succeeded in the conversion of the common folk. Because of the long heritage of Paganism through successive generations, the old ways held firmly in the hearts and minds of the people. Christianity was seen as a sterile religion with some power, some degree of political authority, but no congregation to speak of outside the palace walls.

It was not until the Eighth Century that some real progress was made in converting the people of the land to Christianity. This was when Charlemagne undertook the conquest of the Saxon lands. The conquering general destroyed the Sacred Oak, and offered the newly vanquished a choice between conversion to Christianity and death. To many of the Pagan Saxons, being baptized was a far more attractive choice than being beheaded. But these conversions were, to a great extent, in name only. Their true significance lies in the fact that they gave Christianity a foothold in previously Pagan lands.

By the Tenth Century, all of Western Europe was officially converted to Christianity. Though the old rites of Paganism were performed side by side with Christian ritual, they no longer represented the sole religion of the land. From this point onward, with the new ways finding some degree of acceptance among the Pagan people, the history of Paganism becomes inseparable from the history of the Christian church. Pope Gregory decreed to the clergy that if they found that a belief in the old ways was strong among the populace, and could not dissuade the people from practicing the old rites, they should incorporate them into Christian practice. So it is that seemingly unlikely tales are told of the local bishop leading a fertility dance around the churchyard. These are not the acts of a wayward cleric who'd fallen from grace, but the devout churchman following the edicts of his pope.

Other steps were taken to gather the people to Christian practice. Brigid, the Mother Goddess of Ireland, became canonized, and was recognized as Saint Bridgit. Pagan places of worship were either destroyed or used as the building site for new Christian churches. Much of the strategy employed had some real effect in eliminating the practices of the old religion from the lands.

Still, there was more work to be done before the old ways were banished to memory. For although the outward expressions of Pagan belief had changed, and though the sacred Pagan sites were under Christian control, the hearts of the Pagan people were not sufficiently dissuaded from their dedication to their Gods. So it was time to change tactics to make the transition of the people complete. If the people's love could not be torn from their Gods, then the Gods themselves would be the target of the Christian fathers.

It was now declared heresy to deny the Christian God in favor of the ancient deities of nature. The Christians knew that it was the Horned God in particular who must be unseated in order for them to reign supreme. Therefore, it was now taught that he was, in fact, the same entity as Satan, the Devil of Christian mythology, and that to commune with him would be a punishable offense.

One of the fascinating aspects of these times of persecution lies in a brief analysis of the crime of heresy. Heresy may be defined as nonconformity, dissent, or doctrinal divergence from church dogma. This was liberally interpreted by the Christian fathers in their pursuit of the destruction of the Old Religion. In fact, Nicholas Remy, the author of *Demonolatry*, one of the guidebooks of the witch-hunters, was quoted as saying, "Everything which is unknown lies, as far as I am concerned, in the cursed domain of demonology.... Whatever is not normal is due to the Devil!" This gave the Church a free hand to bring anyone to trial for the smallest slip of the tongue, social lapse, or misinterpreted word or act.

As penalties stiffened for the crime of heresy, and torture became widely accepted as a means for extracting confessions from the wrongdoers, the persecution really got under way. Some have estimated that as many as nine and a half million lives were lost throughout this sad period in history. Certainly, there were many who became victims who were not Pagan. Since the estate of the heretic was divided amongst the church and the magistrates, greed was a factor in the deaths of many.

Those who have chosen to follow Paganism in modern times may refer to this dark period of Pagan history as "the burning times." This is, essentially, a misleading label, for most of the people who were executed as heretics were not burned, but hanged. The phrase, however, survives largely due to the dramatic impact it still holds.

Throughout the persecution, communing with the devil (the Horned God of the Pagans) was seen as a sure sign of witchcraft. Although the crimes are intimately tied with Pagan practice, seldom is the word Pagan used by the magistrates in their descriptions of a victim's crimes. The word "heretic" does appear now and then, but by far, the favorite assessment of the victim of the persecution is "witchcraft."

One of the Bible verses most commonly quoted by even modern-day witch hunters is Exodus 22:18: "Thou shalt not suffer a witch to live." This was taken as a divine sanction for the executions of the times, as well as continued harassment today. However, biblical scholars note that there seems to be some tampering with the original text during translation of the work. The original passage read,

"Thou shalt not suffer a *poisoner* to live." Presumably, it was the age-old knowledge of herbcraft and "potions" held by the remaining Pagans that allowed the fearful populace to swallow this misinterpretation, though the original passage may be interpreted as espousing the sanctity of life, rather than a justification for its annihilation.

In England, the last conviction for heresy or witchcraft was in 1712. In Scotland, it was in 1722. Both countries repealed their laws mandating death for heretics in 1736. In France, executions continued until 1745. In Germany, the last execution took place in 1775. Spain and Switzerland continued to take the lives of convicted heretics until 1781 and 1782, respectively. In Poland, it was not until 1792 that the executions stopped.

After the death penalty was repealed, when the masses were convinced that the world had been saved from the Pagan threat, new laws were made to safeguard the Christian world. Witchcraft was considered less an evil crime, and more a tool for the cunning to entrap the naive. So laws were penned to deal with the trappings of witchcraft, rather than the practice itself. Divination, a common study of Pagan practitioners, became a target. "Fortune-telling" was attacked as a fraudulent practice and declared illegal. In England, these laws remained in effect until 1951.

In modern times, things began to change. Whether it was due to the diminished political power of the Church, or that Paganism was considered irrelevant in our rationalistic, scientific culture, the legal bonds on the old religion fell away. And like a seed that has waited through the harsh winter, the craft began to reemerge.

This liberation set the stage for the resurgence of Pagan practice in our times. Gerald Gardner, an amateur anthropologist, involved himself heavily in researching the old ways of the Pagan people. In 1954, he published the results of his studies. *Witchcraft Today* was one of the earliest books widely available about the old religion.

Mr. Gardner is also known as the founder of the "Gardnerian" tradition of the old religion. Though this is a major accomplishment in itself, it had some other effects that should not be understated. Gerald Gardner, though his work, paved the way for acceptance of those who practiced closely held family traditions. At last, the knowledge that was passed from one generation to the next behind closed doors could be opened to those who were of Pagan mind and Pagan heart.

The first steps taken by Gerald Gardner were furthered by the work of many other individuals. Sybil Leek, a hereditary practitioner, showed the world that the old ways had indeed survived through successive generations of Pagan families. Leo Martello shed light on Italian witches known as the *Strega*. Alex Sanders founded the "Alexandrian" tradition of the craft, and made it accessible to those who would seek to follow the old ways. Raymond Buckland became a key figure in the dissemination of knowledge of the craft, and continues to share the results of his research into his own Romany heritage.

Each of those who have played a part in the early re-emergence of the old ways and who continue to bring Paganism out of the darkness have taken a prominent place in Pagan history. They have helped to inject a note of truth into a public view dominated by fear and superstition. Because of their efforts, those who practice Paganism are much freer to do so than they would have been before this century of knowledge and daring. Although it is true that some of those who have found their way to the public eye are no more than "pop witches," more concerned with their own glory than with the re-opening of the ways of the Gods, each favorable exposure has made it a bit easier for the sincere followers of the old ways.

To be sure, there remains some prejudice to this day. There are those among the Pagan community who have had negative repercussions at their jobs or been rejected among the people of a community or social group. This type of ongoing prejudice does seem to be on the wane, though. And if the Pagan people are not yet free from persecution, at least the life of the Pagan worshiper is no longer on the line. Hopefully, one of the greatest factors in this is a more knowledgeable and sensitive populace.

Organized efforts by Pagan practitioners and sympathizers have also helped. The efforts of Pagan alliances to defend their people have not gone unrecognized. There are activist groups such as the Lady Liberty League, the Coalition for Pagan Religious Rights, Witches Against Relgious Discrimination, the Wiccan/Pagan Press Alliance, and the Wiccan Anti-Discrimination Lobby that have expended great effort to educate Pagans and non-Pagans alike, and to defend against injustice and discrimination wherever they find it.

As knowledge and acceptance of the old ways grows, each Pagan heart hopes for the day when the old Gods and Goddesses can be worshiped in peace. With every effort to amend the ignorance of our pagan roots, that day draws ever closer.

## Chapter Exercises

Imagine yourself a Pagan during the "burning times." Give your imagination free reign. When you've allowed yourself to experience the full scope of what it might have been like to live through the tragedy of this dark period, take another mental journey—this time as an early Christian in the days of Ancient Rome.

## Suggested Additional Reading

*The God of the Witches* by Margaret A. Murray

*Witchcraft Today* by Gerald B. Gardner

# Chapter Two

# *The Nature of the Divine*

Throughout the world's history, religions have spoken of a great force behind and beyond all life, all creation. It is the beginning and the end, the universal truth, the ultimate reality.

The Native Americans know this concept as the "Great Spirit." To the Christian people, it is "God." The followers of Islam call it "Allah," and Buddhists recognize it as simply "the Void."

In trying to define this concept further, we end up with more questions than answers. Christian teachings portray God as an all-powerful being of goodness. He is the Father of all creation. We were created in his image. This seems to offer the beginnings of clarity, but then the questions arise. If God is all-powerful, then why can he not seem to come to terms with the Christian devil and his legions of hell? If he is responsible for all of creation, why would he create for himself such an adversary? If man is created in the image of God, is he also endowed with his virtues? Is God male or female? If God is the Father of Creation, who is the Mother?

The Buddhist concept presents us with a concept of creation proceeding from the Void. This is nebulous enough to allow us to cut through some of the more mundane questions and delve into the realm of the philosopher as we strive toward an understanding of the divine. The laws of physics tell us that although matter can be transformed from one state of existence to another, it cannot be created from nothing. So how could the world as we know it be created from nothingness? From a scientific point of view, the concept of the everything originating in the Void would be invalid.

We seem to be in the precarious position of denying either the laws of physics or the laws of the Creator. Either way, the universe is likely to fly apart! This is the point at which we might make a distinction between spiritual faith and rationalistic knowledge, so that we can determine what we want to direct our own beliefs. The point here is not to take away from the Buddhist concept of the Void, nor deny the Christian God, but to search for truth wherever we might find it.

That being said, let's continue the examination with the Native American concept of the Great Spirit. Many tribes regard the Great Spirit as a creative force, a life force that runs through every living thing. They do not claim to have total understanding, but speak only of what they do know, of what they can see. Though they may mention the Great Spirit, many of the Indian legends do not personify this mysterious force. It is the great mystery of the universe, perhaps beyond mortal understanding. Yet they see the thread of life that permeates everything about them, and they see it as a common bond between all that lives. They strive to develop their limited understanding of the world about them, and turn to nature to better understand the unifying thread of life that flows within them and about them.

This orientation is also the essence of Paganism. Where a Buddhist might accept the Void as a force that can only be seen by the highest consciousness, and accept their ignorance of it as they strive to approach enlightenment, and a Christian might regard the mysteries of the universe simply as a matter of faith, the Pagan seeker is full of questions and a desire to learn more about the world we live in. There is a need to identify with and understand all of nature, to learn to work with the universal order, and in so doing better understand human nature and the nature of the Gods through the common thread of life. In this sense, we are one with each other.

There are, within the framework of Pagan belief, some things that are left to faith. This is the pitfall of many religions. However, the Pagan is not only permitted, but encouraged, to question, learn, compare, and test. It is through these questions that understanding may reach its pinnacle, and faith in the Gods becomes unwavering. Always, the Pagan looks to the world of nature to better know the Pagan Gods.

In all of nature, there are two faces to the life force. They are the male and female principles. We see this manifested in the plants and animals around us, as well as in our own bodies. Some know these forces as the Earth Mother and Sky Father, seeing that male and female forces are each necessary to the creation and continuance of life, and so deify both.

Other traditions in Paganism may recognize these forces by other names, according to their own cultures, mythologies, and folk tales. However, by whatever name these principles are known, their essence remains unchanged. For the purpose of clarity, we will refer to these forces by the common terms God and Goddess.

To take a philosophical view, perhaps these two vital forces are simply different aspects of the same Great Spirit. They seem very distinct and separate, yet interactive and interdependent, acting in unity of purpose. Perhaps these forces are not even truly male and female as we know them. But since we see the reflection of masculine and feminine principles throughout nature, we must relate these lofty concepts to something within our own sphere of understanding.

The God and Goddess can be better seen and understood by recognizing the male and female principles in nature. There is much that can be learned by watching the natural order of things in day-to-day existence. There are cycles that have parallels in our own lives. Through attentive regard of the natural order, we might better understand ourselves, our lives, and the nature of our Gods.

The female and male principles are in evidence throughout nature. In the animal world, for example, each gender has its own role to play and responsibilities to tend—agendas not governed by cultural beliefs as ours are, but by nature's directives. When the male gorilla challenges a stranger that would infiltrate his clan, he is playing out a role dictated by instinct, and thereby fulfilling his true nature. The mare that suckles her newborn foal is acting in accordance with the role designed by nature. Even the pistil and stamen of the plant world are reminiscent of the genital features of their animal counterparts.

Observation of these principles may, indeed, help us to gain a greater understanding of the Divinities and of the universe. But life is more than a spectator sport! We have been given the opportunity to actively experience these truths, rather than simply observe from the outside.

The bonding of a man and a woman can be a sacred act of devotion and understanding. Through deep and spiritual love a man may better come to understand the female nature, and a woman better understand the male nature. On a higher level, through this sacred union, a man might better know the Goddess, and a woman know the God. If the two can sustain a love that is deep and fulfilling, if they can truly be as one, they might grow closer to an understanding of the Great Spirit—the union of the God and Goddess.

It is said that we are spiritually both male and female. We all seek knowledge and the completion of our own natures. To this end, the man-woman relationship is given as a sacred gift from the Gods. Used properly, it can be the perfect tool for learning inner balance, and for growing ever closer to the Divine realm. It is for this reason that the bonding of a man and a woman is held sacred in many Pagan traditions, and treated with the greatest reverence.

The bonding of opposites might be likened to the descent of Persephone into the underworld of Hades in classic Greek myth. Persephone was a maiden, the essence of youth and beauty and joy. Her suitor was the Dark Lord of the land of death. In their union, we may discern a reconciling of light to darkness, of joy to sorrow, innocence to age, and life to death. The dark nature of Hades is softened by the presence of the maiden. The dark deity that is the essence of death embraces Persephone, who is of joy and life. In so doing, the endless cycle of the seasons is established upon the earth, and the promise of rebirth becomes as certain as the inevitability of death.

So too is it with we who dwell in the lands above the dark world of Hades. A man and a woman complete each other's natures through love. The man's harshness is tempered by the gentleness and beauty of his feminine counterpart. Her softness becomes gentle strength when bonded with her lover's nature. They become balanced and are as one. And when their union produces the blessing of children, the promise of continued life becomes as certain as each individual's ultimate journey to the underworld. Strength upon strength in unity yields creation, continuance, and constancy. So the sacred bonding of male and female is not only a key to understanding one's own spirituality, but produces a kinship with the Gods of nature, and brings us to a greater understanding of our deities.

We may also know the God and Goddess through our rites. The Pagan deities are not as lofty as those of some religions. They are not untouchable or unapproachable, nor are they overlords or dictatorial entities that hold the reins to each movement of the universe. They are the essence of the natural world, and inseparable from it. They are also inseparable from human nature and from their worshipers. Pagans can speak to their deities, and they will answer. They are as close as a thought or a wish or a dream, as real as a mountain, a tree, or a running stream.

One of the more confusing aspects of discovering the nature of the God and Goddess is the many names by which they have come to be known throughout different ages and varying cultures. We may hear the Goddess addressed as Cybele, Isis, Demeter, Hecate, Astarte, Marah, or a thousand other names. The God may be known as Marduk, Pluto, Zeus, Bacchus, Cerrunnos, Pan, or a myriad of other names. It should be understood that these names are a human invention, produced by a specific culture in a specific time to refer to a specific aspect or attribute of a deity.

Many Pagans believe that despite the multitude of names, there is but one God and one Goddess. Often, these are broken down into triplicities to foster a better understanding of their natures. The Goddess aspects commonly recognized are separated into three stages of

*The Goddess: Maiden, Mother, Crone*

23

*The God: Young Lord, Warrior, Sage*

24

life. She is seen as the Maiden, the Mother, and the Crone. The God is viewed with parallel aspects in the form of the Young Lord, the Warrior or Protector (a fatherly image), and the Sage or Dark Lord.

The aspects of the male and female principles are a reflection of many of the cycles and changes that are held sacred to the Pagan people. These may be seen in the waxing, full, and waning Moons. They may be recognized in the rising, midday, and setting Sun. These endless cycles reflect the stages of growth that are universal to all of humankind.

Maiden and Young Lord aspects are the essence of birth, growth, and renewal. Their faces are seen in the revitalizing of the earth in spring, in the dark night as the light of the Moon increases from new to full, and in the rising Sun that heralds a new day at dawn. They are seen in the miracle of birth as a new being emerges into the world, and in the child's continued growth as the journey continues from birth to the fullness of manhood or womanhood.

Mother and Warrior are recognized in the fullness of the summer season, when the earth is green and lush with life in its fullness. As the midday Sun ascends overhead casting its brightest rays upon the world, or when the Moon pierces the night with its greatest silver splendor, Mother and Warrior are most visible among us.

The Sage and the Crone embody the wisdom of their many years of life experience. They speak of the restful slowing of life in the waning years as Death claims its due. They are winter, the time of slumber upon the earth, when the green adornment of the land gives way to brown, and at last is covered with a blanket of snow as all the world falls to rest. The Sage and the Crone are the final stop on the cycle of life. They carry Death, but not finality. For in their wisdom, they have watched the cycles of nature turn and turn again. They are the promise of life renewed, of reincarnation and rebirth.

The multiplicity of names for the Pagan deities is for our greater understanding, since we all may find one or more particular face of the God and Goddess easier to relate to than others. But whatever names we choose, they are merely aspects of the male and female forces that permeate all the natural world.

## Pagan Gods and Goddesses

| GOD | GODDESS | CULTURE/TRADITION |
| --- | --- | --- |
| Cerrunnos | Ceridwen | Celtic |
| Apollo | Artemis | Greek |
| Zeus | Hera | Greek |
| Mars | Venus | Roman |
| Odin | Freya | Norse |
| Woden | Frigg | Teutonic |
| Hades | Hecate | Greco-Roman |
| Dagda | Boann | Celtic |
| Llew | Rhiannon | Welsh |
| Lugh | Erin | Irish |

| GOD | GODDESS | CULTURE/TRADITION |
|---|---|---|
| Lucifer | Diana | Italian(Strega) |
| Osiris | Isis | Egyptian |
| Sin | Annit | Chaldean |
| Chandra | Candi | Hindu |
| Wi | Hanwi | Oglala |
| Bohica | Huitaca | Chibicha |
| Amun | Mut | Egyptian |
| Lisa | Mawa | African |
| Tecciztecatl | Coatlicue | Aztec |
| Shen I | Chang O | Chinese |
| Peivalke | Niekia | Russian |
| Tammuz | Ishtar | Babylonian |
| Aningahk | Sedna | Eskimo |
| Endymion | Selene | Greek |
| Khons | Seshat | Egyptian |
| Dionysus | Persephone | Greek |
| Metzli | Coyolxauhqui | Aztec |
| Gwydion | Arianrhod | Welsh |
| Ptah | Hathor | Egyptian |
| Somas | Io | Greek |
| Attis | Cybele | Phrygian |
| Susanowo | Amaratsu | Japanese |
| Anu | Tiamat | Sumerian |
| Cronos | Rhea | Greek |
| Jupiter | Juno | Roman |
| Thoth | Maat | Egyptian |
| Quat | Ro Lei | Melanesian |
| Manannan | Rhiannon | Welsh |

**Chapter Exercises**
Choose a God and a Goddess from a favorite mythology. While reading their adventures, look for examples of how they portray the Young Lord, Father, Sage, Maiden, Mother, or Crone aspects by their actions.

**Suggested Additional Reading**

*The Ancient and Shining Ones: World Myth, Magick & Religion* by D. J. Conway

*The New Book of Goddesses and Heroines* by Patricia Monaghan

*The Sea Priestess* by Dion Fortune

*The Goat-Foot God* by Dion Fortune

Any available writings on your favorite mythology.

# Chapter Three

# *Elements and Elementals*

All of life is made of four basic elements, according to Pagan understanding. They are earth, air, fire, and water. As much as comprising the physical components of creation, these principles embody every phase of life and every human condition. An understanding of the essence as well as the characteristics and workings of each element is the basis of Pagan living, and of all magick. Elemental awareness brings an attunement to the natural order and to the changes within and around us.

Within Pagan religious doctrine (as well as other magickal systems), the four elements are unique and indivisible, yet each a part of the whole that makes up the universe. According to the ancient alchemical writings of Paracelsus, the four elements emanated from the void that was the beginning of creation. Each had distinctive qualities and was an intricate part of the magickal process of the creation. They were each established within their own kingdoms, not one above the other, but each an equally vital part of the universe.

Within the element of earth lay the trees, roots, herbs, fruits, and all the things that grow above and beneath the soil. In fact, the soil itself is of the element of earth. The bounty of this element is manifested in the food that graces our tables as in the harvest of wheat, corn, fruits, and vegetables. The drink that quenches our thirst is often taken from the grape or apple or roots and flowers of the earth. The herbs that flavor our foods and serve as our medicines are from earth as well. That we can depend on our "daily bread" is due to the never-failing ability of the land to produce that which is our food. As such, the essence of earth is stability, constancy, and sustenance. It is all that that is firm and certain. It is truth, honor, and justice. It is the physical world and the study of herbalism.

The element of air has its roots in the non-physical world. It represents that which is unseen. The air is made manifest in the sky that surrounds the physical earth, and provides invisible sustenance to the creatures of the earth with the taking of each breath. It is wind. It is smell. It is thought and knowledge. It is study and beauty, and it is that from which arises the first concept of an artistic pursuit. It is the source of inspiration and poetry.

The element of fire is seen in the Sun, the light of the Moon, and the stars. Barely material in its manifestation, fire is the element of transition and change. It is the drive and determination that lies behind both progress and aggression. It is passion, war, vengeance, and victory. It is warmth, movement, and white-hot fury. It may manifest either as a gentle hearth-fire and warm romance, or as the blaze of a volcano and primal lust.

The element of water manifests as the sea and the dark mystery that resides within its depths. Water is the unseen mystery that lies in the land of death. It is the wonder of universal love as reflected in the expansiveness of the ocean. It is the kingdom of intuition and psychic revelation. It is the great equalizer, in its kingdom of deep power and unending expanse.

Each elemental realm is complete with its own spirits, its own rulers, and its own characteristics. Each functions uniquely within itself, vibrating at its own rate of existence, not unlike the dimensional spheres of science fiction literature. Each realm has a race of beings that is peculiar to its own elemental qualities that exist as a part of, and in support of, the element. Additionally, each living thing is perceived to have a race of elemental spirits to guide and nurture it, or in the case of mountains and rocks, the supposed "inanimate" creatures of the natural world, the elemental spirits help them to "be."Part of the life and understanding of a Pagan practitioner is the contact and appreciation of the spirits of the elemental realms.

While children freely commune and play with the elementals, with age often comes a disposition to blindness in regard to anything not of this plane. The innocence and natural openness of a child's mind makes contact with the elemental spheres a natural event. For us to recapture that ability, it is necessary to step beyond thought, beyond subjective reality, and approach the universe with the eyes of a child, thirsty to drink in all that awaits. Then, though there may be some difficulty in tuning into this realm upon initial attempt, each time a visit is made to the realm of the elemental spirits, the task becomes easier.

Closest to the plane of humankind are the Gnomes, the earth elementals. It is said that these creatures function on a vibratory rate that is closest to that of humans. Gnomes are the personification of the element of earth. The word "gnome" is used here as a broad classification for all of the earth spirits. However, all earth elementals do not have the same characteristics as the traditional gnome. On a journey to the realm of the earth spirits, one might encounter brownies, thornbreaks, and dyads as well as the classical gnome.

Earth elementals often find a place that they make their home, and remain there. Gnomes may have a favorite garden retreat. Dyads may dwell within a particular tree. Thornbreaks may frequent the same brushy hedge. Occasionally, earth elementals may attach themselves to a certain home, or even to a particular person. They may remain at that house or with that individual so long as he or she remains within their good graces. These elementals may be as helpful as they are playful. As often as articles may unaccountably turn up missing, lost items may be retrieved when it is important to find them. Money may also appear in strange places when the need is sincere.

Earth elementals are said to appreciate things that are of the earth. They favor shiny metals, coins, gems, pretty stones, marbles, and seem to respect good craftsmanship. Those who are fortunate enough to have a gnome in their home or garden may place blue marbles or silver coins about for the entertainment of the earth spirits. Many who are hosting house gnomes never pick up loose change should they chance to drop it, but leave it for the enjoyment of their elemental guests.

Air spirits are thought to live in a world of the highest (some say most spiritual) vibratory rate. As such, they are sometimes the last elementals to be seen by the Pagan venturer who steps out into the elemental spheres. Like their earth counterparts, air spirits embody and personify their own element, and are found in places that are of the air.

As a general classification, the spirits of air are known as sylphs. They act to maintain balance within nature and oversee all undertakings of the element of air. They may be discovered in storm clouds, whirl-winds, tornadoes, and hurricanes, as well as in the gentle breeze that cools a summer day. When you see a spiraling breeze whirling the autumn leaves into the air, look for the creatures of air amongst them. A sudden wind on a still night may be the spirits of the air extending their greeting to you.

Among the creatures of air are fairies, aroma sprites (who thrive on the scents carried on the breezes), and the alven. The air spirits tend to have an appreciation of finery. They favor elegant fabrics like silk, especially if it is yellow. Flowers and perfume are gifts that honor them. Keep these things about you if you wish to do them honor.

The most intense of the elemental spirits are those of fire. Known as salamanders, they are the  outlet for the energy that issues from deep within the heart of the earth, as in a volcano spewing hot ash and fiery rock. The fire spirits are the guiding force and essence of this deep flame. In some ways, they may be considered the purest of all elemental spirits. Where it is difficult to imagine a gnome as a being composed of pure earth or rock, or a sylph as a being made up of air, salamanders are fire in body as well as in essence. It is fire that they are about, and it is fire that honors them.

There is no better way to please the salamanders than to build a fire for them. Alternately, the fire elementals might appreciate something that is dedicated to their element. Leave them a stone that embodies the essence of fire, such as volcanic obsidian, or cornelian, red as true fire. Set out some fiery herbs like myrrh or cinnamon. Better yet, prepare an incense from the herbs and burn it in their honor. Play some music that captures the intensity of the flame, and let them dance among the hearth fire as it plays.

The element of water completes the primal foursome. The water spirits exist in a world that rolls and flows like the easy rhythm of the waves of the ocean. These creatures of water are known as undines. Like the other spirits of the elemental realms, undines are the personification of their element. They are behind the rise and fall of the tides. They are in the currents of the flowing rivers and streams, and may be seen on the crests of the waves as they roll in from the great expanse of the ocean. They store and release energy into the natural order, as well as support and sustain the creatures who dwell within the waters of the earth.

Some of the different types of water elementals are water sprites, nixies, kelpies, and water babies. Their enjoyment of water is so complete that they may tend to forget, when you visit them, that you are not of their realm. Some have reported that the water spirits kept them a long time swimming and playing in the waters, until breath and strength were all but drained from them. It is almost as if there is a lack of understanding how any being who loves the water could quit its comfort. Captured by their enchantments, a visiting Pagan may find the water spirits as potentially devastating as they are delightful.

Water elementals appreciate things of beauty, especially those reminiscent of the water. One might honor them by leaving blue beads, moonstones, cones of mother of pearl, or gifts of silver.

Together, these are the forces behind all of nature. Although each is evident within its own realm, and most apparent in the body of its own element, they work together to make the natural world complete. They are, to some extent, always present together in every form of life. The fire cannot burn without wood from the earth to feed it, nor the air to help it breathe. The basin of the ocean floor is formed of the sands of the earth. During times of storm, the strong gales are inseparable from the rains they carry, and the fiery lightning must also play its part. The plants of the earth drink deeply of the waters to sustain themselves, and turn their faces to the fires of the sun. The seeds that will bring future generations of plants are carried on the wings of the air.

## Elemental Qualities and Associations

| EARTH | AIR | FIRE | WATER |
|-------|-----|------|-------|
| North | East | South | West |
| Stability | Intellect | Courage | Love |
| Strength | Wisdom | Passion | Emotion |
| Pentacle | Wand | Sword | Cup |
| Green | Yellow | Red | Blue |
| Brown | Gray | Yellow | Green |
| Midnight | Dawn | Noon | Dusk |
| Winter | Spring | Summer | Autumn |
| Law | Life | Light | Love |
| Reason | Faith | Hope | Charity |
| Old Age | Childhood | Youth | Maturity |
| Venus | Mercury | Sun | Moon |
| Friday | Wednesday | Sunday | Monday |
| Gnome | Sylph | Salamander | Undine |
| Oakmoss | Mimosa | Myrrh | Cypress |
| Patchouli | Violet | Cinnamon | Clove |

While each element is pure within itself, it requires the others to sustain the natural order of the universe.

The wise Pagan sees the wonder of each in its own right, but also honors them in their unity. It is this unity that is the essence of all creation and continued life and rebirth.

**Chapter Exercises**

1. Spend a day with each of the elements in turn. Enter into a meditation with each of the elements. Surround yourself with that which is of the element. For example, a visit to the sea at dusk for water, or going high upon a hill at dawn for air, in the forest at midnight for earth, and at midday before a campfire for fire. Learn what you can about each.

2. As you walk among nature, be open to the appearance of elemental spirits. When the water ripples in a still lake, is it the chance movement of a fish, or the water play of an undine? When the autumn leaves are swept up from the earth and swirled about in a whirlwind, is it a chance breeze, or the frolic of air fairies?

3. Choose an everyday object. Examine it carefully. Think about it. How much of each element is in its make-up? What about yourself? Are you more attuned with one element than another? Think not only of physical characteristics, but of the qualities and virtues of each of the elemental realms.

**Suggested Additional Reading**

*Gnomes* by Wil Huygen and Rien Poortvliet

*The Real World of Fairies* by Dora van Gelder

*Earth Power* by Scott Cunningham

*An Encyclopedia of Fairies* by Katherine Briggs

# Chapter Four

# *Craeft Traditions*

Throughout the years, many different traditions have arisen within the old religion. Several factors have been responsible for the advent of different expressions of Pagan belief.

Geographic and cultural differences can account for some of the differences. The need for secrecy during the time of persecution is also a factor. Practicing Pagans in those times withdrew into small, close-knit circles, the intention being the protection of all Pagans from those who would seek them out and extract their confessions through torture. Unfortunately, one of the results of this was the loss of contact with others who shared a kinship in their practice of the old ways. Much of the knowledge that may have been shared between circles was lost as each individual unit developed whatever knowledge and ritual they had, and altered and augmented their own practices in accordance with their own needs and circumstances.

Today, Paganism survives in many varying forms throughout the world. These early traditions have since been expanded by some modern interpretations of the old religion. Many elements of ritual work are shared throughout different current forms of Pagan worship, although there are some that are peculiar to certain traditions, or held in higher regard in some than in others.

Two of the most recently developed and widely known traditions are the Gardnerian and Alexandrian. The Gardnerian tradition receives its name from Dr. Gerald Gardner, who, through his studies in anthropology and his own personal research, attempted to step back in time to recapture the Pagan worship that had once been the way of the people. Much had been lost through time, but his efforts uncovered many hints of the old religion as it was practiced in times past.

Gardnerians are matriarchal in their worship. The Goddess is their supreme deity, and the High Priestess, as her earthly representative, is supreme in their rituals. According to the tradition as originally laid out by its founder, Gardnerians enter into their rites "sky-clad," or without clothing. (However, many modern Gardnerian covens do work robed.) They also practice ritual scourging for purification. Scourging is the practice of ritual flagellation for the purpose of exorcising all negativity from an individual so that they may enter into the sacred rites pure of mind and heart. For many covens, the scourge is constructed of a very light silken thread, and scourging is a symbolic act, not intended to inflict pain, but to illustrate the individual's willingness to sacrifice and become pure and clean in the face of the deities.

The Alexandrian tradition was developed by Alex Sanders. According to his own presentation of his personal history, Alex Sanders was initiated into the practice of the Old Religion by his grandmother. This would indicate that he is originally of a hereditary tradition. However, he trained extensively in the Kabbalah and in ceremonial magick. These are the practice of systems rooted in the Judeo-Christian approach to religious ceremony and magick. Elements of these studies have been incorporated into the Alexandrian rites and passed on to others in their training. The addition of material from these other magickal systems makes the resulting tradition developed by Alex Sanders unique.

There are many parallels between the rites of the Alexandrians and Gardnerians. Like the followers of Gardner, Alexandrians are also a matriarchal tradition. They also make use of the scourge for ritual purification, and tend to work sky-clad, although the High Priest and High Priestess have the option of dressing as they wish.

There is one point that remains in controversy regarding the Alexandrian ritual practices. Many traditions practice a wine blessing, or symbolic bonding of the male and female forces of nature. This is known among many traditions as the Great Rite. In most traditions, the Priest holds a knife, symbolic of the male, and the Priestess holds a chalice of wine, representing the female. The knife is inserted into the cup in a symbolic gesture representing the male and female coming together, their union being the force of creation.

The controversy arises with ritual photographs of Alex Sanders in the midst of this symbolic bonding. It is not the Priestess, but Alex Sanders as the priest who is seen holding the chalice, while the Priestess handles the knife. It has been wondered how this odd departure from the norm originated. Some have guessed that since the photographs in question were taken in the earliest days of public working, that Alex

**The Wine Blessing: Knife and Chalice**

Sanders reversed this rite to preserve the traditional secrecy of Pagan worship. In fact, he has since been seen performing this same rite in private ritual in a manner that is more congruent with the practices of other traditions.

Many of the other Pagan traditions fall under the general category of "traditional." Some of these traditions are Welsh, Nordic, Teutonic, or Celtic. What sets these groups apart from others is that they cling to the mythology and culture of a chosen people. The Welsh traditionalists, for example, practice their rites in accordance to the ways and legendry of Wales. The mythology they hold dear is derived from the *Mabinogion*. They call to their deities with the same names used by the Pagans of old Wales who went before them. Their rites may be spoken in part, or completely in the Welsh tongue.

Members of Celtic, Nordic, Teutonic, or any other traditionalist groups parallel the workings of the Welsh in that their mythology is rooted in the history of a certain culture, and they would incorporate the customs, practices, and perhaps the language of the particular people into their rites.

There are, additionally, some groups that are related to the traditionalists, but tend to concentrate on a selected facet of a culture, or of a specific time in the history of a people. Such examples are the Celtic Faery traditions, or the Nordic Viking groups. Their mythology is a bit less general, but relates to a given period in the mythological history of a people, or a specific mythological cycle in the changing legendry of a culture.

Hereditary or family traditions are not divided along lines of culture or legend, but by ancestry. Knowledge of the old religion is passed down through family members. In some families, it is passed to only one person in each successive generation. Some pass down the family practices to every alternate generation. Within my own tradition, the practice of the old ways was passed from Grandmother to

Granddaughter. It was chiefly the responsibility of the women to keep the religion alive through successive generations. So while the men within the family tended to worldly concerns, the women held to the religion, and passed on the knowledge of the old ways to each successive generation. Unfortunately, though it must have seemed like a good approach at the time, the elders of the family looked around one day and found that the training of the men within the Pagan way had been sorely neglected, and while the females of the tradition had held tightly to the sacred path, there were no priests to complement their work, and the tradition was out of balance. It was at this point that the approach to training and passing on the old ways was altered. We are now a tradition that believes strongly in balance and in the practice of working man to woman and woman to man.

Many hereditary families take a less ritualistic approach to their religion in the way that they practice Paganism. Classes are often far less formal, inasmuch as a walk with Grandma in the woods can reveal as much insight as a formal lecture. There is a natural familiarity between student and teacher. Trust is ingrained, and need not be developed, but is an easy foundation for the beginnings of faith. Every gathering of the clan is an opportunity to learn, to commune with nature, and to worship the Gods. So while there is no less devotion in family tradition, there is often far less formality in the approach to the old religion.

Just as Alexandrians can trace the lineage of their initiation to Alex Sanders, and Gardnerians to Dr. Gardner, hereditary Pagans look back to their family tree. There are some who can trace their Pagan ancestry with certainty as far back as 700 years or more. The hereditary traditions hold the knowledge of ancient rites and customs observed by their families for generations, including spells, healing, and systems of magick and training that may have been practiced in ancient times.

In this century, one of the most recognizable examples of a hereditary Pagan is Sybil Leek. Among the most fascinating experiences in my own life was meeting this "legend." She was a grand lady, a friend, and a peacemaker of whom I carry many pleasant memories since she has passed on. She was also, as few might expect, very down to earth and straightforward.

While Sybil chose to become public in her practice of the old ways, her mother continued her creaft traditions in private. Upon our meeting, she presented herself as a sweet Grandmotherly type, and she seemed to have an air of the wisdom of an Elder about her. She was to prove as inspiring to me as her famous daughter.

The blending of wisdom and universal love this woman embodied captures the essence of family practice, through which love of the Gods extends to love of fellow humankind. More modern traditions express this same feeling as "Perfect Love and Perfect

Trust." It may not always be a perfect world, but the Pagan people, fortified with the love of their Gods and each other, strive to make it so.

While discussing the family traditions, it would seem appropriate to mention one of the more interesting aspects of their recent history. There was a time, within the last twenty-five years or so, that to be of hereditary background was considered to be a badge of honor. Some believed that it reflected a greater quality or higher knowledge than some of the more recently developed or rediscovered traditions. This awe of family tradition even engendered false claims of a hereditary background among prestige-seekers.

In fact, it seems that those who were least impressed with the fact of being from a family tradition were the hereditaries themselves. I recall one Priestess, trained by her grandmother, who used to purposely understate her station to those who were impressed by status and tradition. When asked if she were a High Priestess, she would reply simply, "I'm a Pagan." In fact, she was not only hereditary, but one of the finest, most capable Priestesses with whom I've ever had the privilege to work.

In recent years, this has all become much less of an issue. We would hope that this represents the reflection of a note of truth, tolerance, and love, a bonding of the Pagan people. In fact, if seen clearly, the hereditaries are in very much the same position as Pagans from other traditions. Members of the newer traditions are in the position of gathering what they can from ancient practices. The family practitioners hold the keys to many rites that have survived through time—but as much as may have survived the rigors of time, much has also been lost. So to some extent, the family practitioners are also searching for lost knowledge. In addition, Paganism is a living religion—always changing, always growing. Few Pagans would turn their backs on a particularly effective piece of ritual, or a deeply insightful bit of knowledge. In our ignorance, as well as our knowledge, the Pagan people have much in common. One tradition cannot be placed above another.

Many of today's groups would fall under the general classification of "eclectic." These are practices that have been established by gathering bits and pieces of knowledge and ritual from wherever it became available. Little bits of knowledge and ritual pieces might be taken from a number of different traditions and incorporated into a sincere and workable expression of Pagan practice.

One of the other types of Pagan worship that may be seen today incorporates the needs and desires of a select group of practitioners. These groups are not necessarily formed along the lines of a particular culture, but are directed toward the character of those who become members. One such group is the homosexual coven. There are some of these groups that are practicing the rites of a homosexual priesthood from ancient times. Others are homosexual by personality, choice, or desire, and feel most comfortable working with people of a similar orientation. These groups may adhere to any cultural tradition.

There is another type of Pagan practitioner that should not be overlooked. This is the solitary, the lone practitioner of the old religion. Unlike some of the other traditions, this group has always been in evidence, probably always will be, and is ever-growing in its numbers.

A solitary is one who follows the old ways on their own rather than bonding to a coven or a working group. The reason for following their chosen path in solitude is their own. It may range from living in a secluded area where transportation to the nearest covenstead is difficult, to a personal preference for communing with their Gods in private.

There are some who would object that many solitaries practice their rites in accordance with what they've learned in books and throughout their own lives, but never have the guidance of a teacher or the benefit of an initiation. In some respects, this may be an obstacle to the solitary practitioner. However, the need for secrecy is not as severe as it has been in times past, and not every Pagan wants to be or needs to be initiated into the priesthood. To have all priests and no one to minister to results in a sterile priesthood. It robs the office of the priesthood of purpose.

Whatever tradition is most suited to the individual, there are certain guidelines that are somewhat universal that could prove helpful in making a decision whether or not to affiliate with a working group, and in choosing which group might be most appropriate. For one thing, many covens have some sort of initiation or induction ritual upon becoming a member. The nature of these rites may vary from one group to the next, but the tone they take can offer a good deal of insight into the workings of the individual group or coven.

One of the things to watch for is the exchange of money. Although it is not unreasonable to ask reimbursement for the costs of materials used in training, there should be no charge for initiation or for the training itself. A group may ask you to pay for your own working tools, but there should be no charge for the actual initiation. A true initiation can only be bought with the sincerity and dedication of the seeker. All the money in the world is of no account if these virtues are lacking.

On the other side of the fence, it is a privilege and an obligation of the priesthood to offer teaching and training in the ways of the old Gods to the devout seeker. It should never be a quest for profit. The benefits reaped in the training of a sincere Pagan should go to the glory of the Gods and the common good of the Pagan people, not to the pocketbook of the trainer or initiator. Those who encounter a request for unreasonable charges and fees should run as quickly as they can in the opposite direction, since the sincerity and integrity of the would-be initiator is highly suspect.

Most traditions recognize a duality of creation in the form of a God and Goddess. While some revere one above the other, others believe in perfect balance between the two. However, regardless of the doctrine of a particular tradition, the duality is apparent in most legitimate traditions, most traditions rooted in sincere practice of the old ways.

Rituals are held with regard to the changing cycles of nature. All traditions celebrate the ways of nature in some respect, often centering on rites attuned to solar or lunar cycles. In fact, reverence for nature and our part in it is largely the essence of Paganism.

The Old Religion is a celebration of life. As such, there is no place for sacrifice of any living creature. While it is true that our Pagan ancestors were more given to offering sacrifice to the Gods, this has been acknowledged by most modern practitioners of the Old Religion as unnecessary as well as unkind.

When choosing a coven or a working group, be discerning. The guidelines listed here should be evident in most Pagan practices. If there are differences, do not be afraid to question. If an individual is asked or required to do anything that makes them uncomfortable or feel violated in any way, they may be in the wrong group. There are some covens that still hold to the ways of secrecy. These may scrutinize a candidate very closely before admission to the group is either granted or denied. It is the right and obligation of the individual to screen the group as carefully. The only good alliance is a mutually agreeable and beneficial one.

Another point to be made in choosing a group is to keep your eyes and heart open, as well as your ears. No matter what any individual representative has to say about their own way of Pagan practice, no matter what attractive promises they might make, note well whether or not their actions bear out their words. One who speaks of love and balance and harmony should not go home and beat their children. Note their actions well, not only with you, who they may be "romancing," but with those around them. Do they have the love and respect of those around them? Have they earned it?

The division of the Pagan people into varied traditions and different covens has had numerous benefits. A great feeling of love and trust and loyalty can arise among the members of a close group—a feeling that may be one of the factors in the survival of the old religion through a very difficult history. Many traditions welcome their adherents into a circle after an expression of "Perfect Love and Perfect Trust." Although this is as much an ideal as a reality, many tightly bonded groups feel these principles between themselves and in communion with the God and

Goddess as perfectly as anyone may be able. As an aside, a High Priestess whom I deeply respect once suggested that we might consider no longer talking of the ideal as if we have already attained it, but begin speaking of perfecting love, and perfecting trust.

Unfortunately, to invert a phrase, every silver lining has a cloud inside it. So has it been with the separation of Pagans into different traditions. The loyalty and unity within each group has, sometimes, kept the Pagan people apart from one another. Different ways of doing things are too easily labeled right or wrong, black or white, good or bad, instead of being kept in perspective. In fact, what they are, in most cases, is merely different.

In addition, there are some groups who measure their success in numbers rather than quality. How many initiations one has handed out can become more important to the misguided Priest or Priestess than the validity of those initiations—more important than the service rendered to the God, Goddess, and the Pagan people through the vehicle of initiation. Combined with the inherent differences between traditions, this has given rise to endless arguments between groups, one tradition vying for power or people over another, and constant senseless bickering. In the early 1970s, the term "bitchcraft" was coined to appropriately characterize this situation. It is of little consequence whether the divisions among Pagan people arise out of a deep-rooted belief in a single tradition, or for the gratification of the ego of one individual or another—the situation remains counter-productive.

There is no single way that is the only way. If there were, then any alternative traditions would soon die out as impractical and unworkable. Yet there are many Pagan traditions that continue to survive, to thrive, and to do well by their adherents. Separated from one another, coiled and ready to spring in attack, the Pagan people can only hope to bring disunity to their worship. And each attack would seem to demand a counter-attack, until the situation degenerates into a never-ending circle of constant battle. But think what the Pagan people could accomplish in unity! Consider the knowledge that might be shared, the good work that might be accomplished, and the glory that may be delivered to the Pagan God and Goddess by a unified people.

**Chapter Exercises**

Consider the benefits of working solitary or in unison with a group. At this point in your development, which would be more beneficial to you? Which would you prefer?

**Additional Suggested Reading**

*Witchcraft Today* by Gerald Gardner

*The Alex Sanders Lectures* by Alex Sanders

*Scottish Witchcraft: The History and Magick of the Picts* by Raymond Buckland

*Witta: An Irish Pagan Tradition* by Edain McCoy

*Celtic Magic* by D. J. Conway

*Rites of Odin* by Ed Fitch

*The Quest* by Ruddlum Gawr

*The Tree: The Complete Book of Saxon Witchcraft* by Raymond Buckland

*To Ride a Silver Broomstick: New Generation Witchcraft* by Silver Ravenwolf

*Aradia: Gospel of the Witches* by Charles G. Leland

# Chapter Five

## *Esbats and Rites of Passage*

The word "esbat" is derived from the Old French word *esbattre* which means "to frolic and amuse oneself." This word may have endured through the centuries due to its descriptive value.

The rites of Paganism are, very much, celebrations of life. The meaning of the word *esbat* embraces the essence of what a celebration is.

In modern times, convenience and legal and social constraints have had the effect of altering traditional observance of Pagan rites. Many groups hold monthly, semi-monthly, or weekly meetings which they know as their esbats. To these Pagans, esbat has come to mean any gathering that is not in honor of one of the major festivals, or Sabbats.

Other more traditional groups gather at the time of the full Moon and new, or dark Moon. These days are observed because they mark one of the most readily visible cycles of nature, and Paganism, in its truest sense, is a celebration of nature. It is through nature that we survive, and through our attunement to nature that we might better gain an understanding of ourselves, the world around us, and the essence of the divine.

According to the old lore as presented in Leland's *Gospel of the Witches,* it was an issue from the lips of the Goddess herself that the Pagans should "once in every month, and better it be when the Moon is full" pay their respects to the God and Goddess. The phases of the Moon are of special significance to the followers of the old ways. Within its cycles, the Pagan people see the reflection, and, some believe, the essence of their Goddess. As the Moon changes from dark to crescent to full, Pagans are reminded of the

Crone, Maiden, and Mother aspects of the Goddess. The aspect honored in the esbat ritual as well as the tone that the rites may take may be a reflection of the lunar phase. For example, when the Moon is in waxing Crescent, there may be a petition for love or growth. The Full Moon may honor childbirth or healing, and the Dark Moon may find the rites petitioning the Crone for greater wisdom. In many traditions among the Pagan community, the cycles of the Moon are a foundation of esbat observance.

This is not to take away from the validity of nontraditional esbat rites. The world is not as it once was. Those who follow the ways of nature often cannot do so without regard to the social ways of the world. They have jobs to consider, schools for their children, and a thousand other demands on their daily lives. In addition, there are those groups that have developed into formal Pagan temples. There are often legal criteria to be observed (such as a mandate that a legal religious organization meet regularly once a week) in order to retain their legal status as a religion.

However, if we are to offer an accurate overview of Pagan practice, it is important to discuss the reasons for, and benefits of the traditional observances of the esbats. Within the cycles of the Moon there seems to appear a sort of psychic power surge. Those of a more sensitive nature can feel the energy as it ebbs and flows. In attuning oneself to the flow of the lunar energy tides, one becomes more in tune with the natural order-and perhaps a bit closer to the realm of the Divine.

In ritual work, the Pagan people take advantage of the Moon flows. The added boost of energy that is evident as the Moon travels through its cycles can be tapped through ritual and redirected toward some worthy purpose, such as the bonding of people in peace, or a healing of one in need. Pagans look forward to the rise and fall of the Moon's fullness. This natural cycle is a source of attunement, power, life, and elation.

As highly as the Pagan people regard this natural power surge, however, there are others who are just as wary of it. For those who are not in tune with the ways of nature, this lunar power surge can manifest as a kind of nervous energy that is sometimes expressed in a negative manner. Police departments throughout the world have compiled statistics that reflect an unexplained rise in criminal activity on nights when the Moon is full. Many, as a matter of normal procedure, increase the number of officers on duty as the Moon waxes full. In addition, the Moon has long been associated with the realm of the subconscious and with psychic energy. The root word of lunacy is *luna*, Latin for moon. In hospitals, there has been some evidence collected that indicates an excessive amount of bleeding in surgical procedures at the Full Moon. Ocean tides rise and fall with the cycles of the Moon. If the movements of the lunar orb can have effects on something as large as the ocean, why not in the realm of human existence?

These are but a few of the manifestations of the lunar power cycle. In a Pagan circle, in an atmosphere of understanding and respect for the natural order, the power tides can be used to increase the level of learning and development, or they can be channeled into the creation of positive ends. Without understanding, this is wild, uncontrolled energy, and the police and other authorities have their hands full!

As far as the practical ritual application of the changing Moon is concerned, the Dark Moon and Full Moon each have their own dominions. The New Moon is considered a time of endings and new beginnings. As one cycle comes to a close, the next one begins. This is a time for the completion of projects, and the initiation of new ones. The key word for the Full Moon is "fulfillment." Many favor this time for spells of love, of working magick so that their hearts might be fulfilled. It is also a time for rites of health and success, and a time for thanksgiving. As the lunar light grows full, so have many of the desires and needs of the Pagan people come to fruition. This is a time to appreciate the bounty received, and to give thanks to the God and Goddess for their love and guidance.

Through the years, traditions have carried names and legends for each Moon cycle. Each Moon bears a name descriptive of the time of the year in which it rises. The lunar legends are like a Pagan catechism by which we become attuned with the world about us. Depending on culture and geographic location, the lunar cycles may bear different names. Those that appear below are the ones used by some Pagan groups in the United States and Canada. They seem to be somewhat of a mix between European and North American culture. However, there are many others that are used by groups with other cultural background. Those traditions with significant Native American influence may take their names from the culture of a particular tribe.

The first Moon of the Pagan year, according to many traditions, rises in October, just before the celebration of All Hallows, or Samhain (October 31). This, then, is a sampling of the Moon lore that stands behind the Pagan year:

The *Blood Moon* rises in October, the first Moon before All Hallows' (November 1). It is associated with the color red, and reflects the time of the slaughter of the animals, of stockpiling food for the coming winter season. In many climates, the temperature has dropped enough to permit the preservation of meat. As the first frost is not far away, plant life will soon disappear from the earth, and meat becomes the major source of food throughout the winter.

The *Snow Moon* is the Moon of November. It is associated with a pale blue-silver color. In this time, if the first snow has not already fallen, it is not far away. The earth begins a time of slumber beneath the blankets of snow, gathering strength for the new life at the reawakening of spring.

The *Oak Moon* arrives in December. It is considered a black Moon, and is associated with the Dark Lord aspect of the Pagan God. The oak, as his symbol, is the wood traditionally burned in the Yule fire.

The *Ice Moon* (or Wolf Moon) comes in January. Its color is purple, and its legend recounts how the waters of the earth are imprisoned beneath a sheet of ice, much as Persephone of Greek legend is locked in the underworld as death and winter reign.

The *Storm Moon* describes the long awaited movement of the frozen waters. As the rains fall and the oceans rage, it is a certain sign that the waters will flow once more, and spring return to the lands of the earth. This Moon is associated with the color blue, the color of the waters. It rises in February, and is often dedicated to the Goddess Brigid.

The *Chaste Moon* reflects the release of Persephone from the land of death. It is the return of spring with life renewed. It is virginal-fresh, clean, and untouched. Appropriately, its color is white. It rises in March.

The *Seed Moon* heralds the growth that will color the earth as the season advances. The seeds that lay sleeping beneath the soil begin to stir, as all of life awakens to the warming earth. Its color is light green, and it comes to us in April.

The *Hare Moon* rises in May. It is dedicated to the Goddess and to fertility. Pink, the color of love, is also the color of the Hare Moon. As spring reaches its height, the thoughts of each young man and maid turn to romance.

The *Dyad Moon* is the Moon that rises around the time of the Summer Solstice in June. Dyad, an old word meaning "pair," reflects the visible presence of the God and Goddess reflected in the bright sun and green fields. This Moon is considered orange, the color of the summer sun.

The *Mead Moon* rises in July. It is the last Moon before the harvest, and is celebrated with dancing and song. This is the time when the Pagans of old made the mead for the coming harvest celebration. Mead Moon is yellow, the color of the rich honey mead that is being prepared at its rising.

The *Wort Moon* is the dark green Moon of August. Wort, a word known to our ancestors to describe the greenery of the earth, is the name given to the Moon that rises as the plants are about to be harvested. This is the time to give honor to the fruits that fill our bellies, for the time of their ending will arrive with the first sweep of the scythe at harvest time.

The *Barley Moon* rises before the Fall Equinox in September. The grains are harvested. It is the end of the season, and the end of the yearly cycle. Brown, the color of grain, is the color of the Barley Moon.

The *Wine Moon* is the odd Moon of the year. With the changing of the lunar calendar to a solar one, there is an overlap in some months. There are sometimes twelve Moons that rise in the solar year, and sometimes thirteen. When this extra Moon rises, it is usually placed in September or October, often just before the Blood Moon. This Moon honors wine, considered the first luxury given by the Gods. It is the time when wine is made for use in the cold winter ahead. Its color is purple-red or burgundy, the color of wine.

The observance of the esbats is full of tradition, history, and Pagan lore. These are times of reflection as well as celebration. It is no wonder so many find fulfillment in riding the lunar tides.

In addition to the cycles in the world about them, Pagans celebrate the changing phases of their own lives. There are several key times in the life of the Pagan man or woman that reflect their own growth and development, and are welcomed with appropriate ritual observance. These are the rites of passage, the transition from one state of being to another. Those most commonly celebrated are birth, Pagan dedication, initiation, hand-fasting, and death.

Unlike those who believe in the doctrine of Original Sin, the great majority of Pagans do not feel that there is need of a spiritual cleansing at birth. It is a welcoming of the newly arrived children to the world. They come to life to learn, to love, and often, to teach others. Pagan ritual does not tie the newly born child to the old religion, but asks the protection, the blessing, and guidance of the God and Goddess for the new arrival. The child is welcomed into the world with any appropriate songs, chants, talismans, and gifts. Often, a natal astrology chart is presented to the parents of the child upon his or her birthing ritual.

As a child grows and learns the ways of the old religion, he or she might wish to make a commitment to the Pagan way of life. Paganing, or dedication, formalizes a person's commitment to study the ways of the religion, to keep the sabbats and esbats, and to strive to grow ever closer to their God and Goddess.

Although there are different versions of this ritual among varying traditions, the intentions are generally the same. Often, there are questions put to the candidate for Paganing to test their resolve to follow the Old Ways with sincerity. If answered satisfactorily, the candidate is granted admission to the circle. Then there is a blessing with the elements, vows of continued study and worship are made, and often a Pagan name is given to mark this new phase in the newly committed Pagan's life.

Another important step in the development of many Pagans is initiation. In some traditions, initiation is a commitment to the continued study of the old ways and to the honor of the God and Goddess. Within some Pagan groups, it is a promise to keep the honor of the Deities and the confidences of the tradition. It is a promise of loyalty. Some of these traditions will offer no teaching until such a commitment is made. Still other traditions initiate only after a certain level of training has already been completed. For these groups, initiation is, essentially, the elevation of an individual to the level of priesthood. In this case, a substantial level of understanding and commitment must be realized before the thought of initiation will be seriously entertained. This is a very important step as it expands the sphere of responsibility from commitment to their own progress and development, to helping others to learn and grow.

Different traditions have different levels of initiation, and different criteria for ascending to each progressive level. It should be remembered, in any case, that initiation is not the right path for everyone. Paganism is, primarily, a religion of the people. Not everyone is right for priestly responsibilities, nor should they feel obligated to travel that path.

One tradition's approach to and criteria surrounding the rites of initiation may differ significantly from another's. Having had the opportunity to discuss initiation with Priests and Priestesses from varying traditions, I found there are certain key areas of contention. Some honor self-initiation, while others consider this an act of dedication only. Some consider initiation to be an act of growth within the old religion, while others consider it a prerequisite to enter into the old ways. Many of those who believe in an initiatory priesthood (i.e., not self-initiation) hold firmly to this view because of their belief in a need for formal training. And while Gardnerians welcome a new initiate into the old religion as "Priest/ess and witch," and other traditions share this view of initiation as elevation to priesthood, to some it is a rite of personal commitment to the old religion, but not a bond of obligation.

There are other rites, however, that are more universally enjoyed. When fortune smiles, and love abounds, many find that one special person with whom they wish to offer their love and life. The hand-fasting or marriage rite is devoted to making that commitment of love, and asking the blessing of the God and Goddess on the couple's union. The actual hand-fasting ritual may take many forms. There may be an exchange of vows and handfasting rings. The couple may jump a broom, a symbol of fertility, to ensure that their own relationship is fruitful. The couple may be bound hand to hand (hence, "hand-fasting") as a symbol of their commitment to live together as one, supportive of each other and of their union. There are provisions within some traditions to set a limit of a lunar year (a year and a day) on the hand-fasting. At the end of this time, should the couple agree, it can be renewed. In other rites, the couple is bound for life.

The ritual bonds established by the hand-fasting can be severed, should it become necessary, by a "parting of the ways," or hand-parting rite. However, vows made within the circle and in the presence of the deities are not to be broken lightly or without due thought. Every effort should be made to keep that commitment, every chance at reconciliation pursued. This is true whether that commitment is for the passing of the lunar year, or the couple is bound heart to heart and hand to hand for life.

The final rite of passage is the death rite, or passing on. This ritual dispels all earthly ties, and delivers the spirit of the departed into the divine realm. This rite may also be performed when an earth-bound spirit is encountered; that is, a spirit who has passed from life, but has not continued onward in his or her spiritual journey and remains tied to the physical world as if it were yet a part of his or her existence. The death rite is designed to make passing on to the next phase of existence easier.

In addition to rites of passage, there are some special purpose rituals that may be undertaken. These rites may include: cleansing after a particularly unpleasant physical, mental, or emotional trauma; sealing; protection; calming; or healing. Whatever the purpose, if the need is great, the Pagan can use ritual work to call on the help of their God and Goddess. Any competent working Priest or Priestess should be able to ritually satisfy the demand, whatever the particulars of the situation.

## Chapter Exercises

Try your hand at "Riding the Moon." During the next Moon cycle, keep a journal of the things that happen in your life; the upswings and the down. Write down how you react to different situations, how you feel, when you feel empowered. At the top of the page, do not keep dates, but lunar phases. Note specifically Waxing Crescent, Full Moon, Waning Crescent, and Dark Moon. When the cycle is over, review your journal. Note how you reacted differently to similar situations during different phases of the Moon. Then try it for another cycle, this time armed with the insights you've gained from your first Moon Ride. In time, you' ll find that you'll ride the power tides like the crest of a wave, rather than being tossed about in the currents.

## Additional Suggested Reading

*Moon Magick: Myth & Magick, Crafts & Recipes, Rituals & Spells* by D. J. Conway

*Moon Lore: Myths and Folktales from Around the World* by Gwydion O' Hara

*Lady of the Night: A Handbook of Moon Magick and Rituals* by Edain McCoy

*Celebrating Life* by Tzipora Klein

# Chapter Six

# *The Sabbats*

In addition to the esbats, or lesser celebrations, most Pagan circles observe eight major festivals throughout the year. Although they are known by different names in different practices, these celebrations usually occur on or about the same date. Many of these are still noted on non-Pagan calendars, and have been remembered by many in holiday celebrations throughout the centuries. They do, however, have their roots in the Pagan practices of days past.

At the end of October, Halloween is still observed throughout many lands. This is the time of the Pagan festival of Hallowmas, Samhain, West Wind Sabbat, or The Festival of World's-Meet. At this time, the veil that separates the world of the living and the world of spirit is considered to be at its thinnest. At Samhain, this veil is held aside, and the spirits of ancestors, family, and loved ones are invited to join in the celebration. It is a renewal of family bonds, a reliving of past loves, and a communion with those who walked a Pagan path in the ages before our birth. Some groups observe the Feast of the Dead. Salt, bread, pork, and apples may be left on the doorstep for the indulgence of the departed spirits.

This is one of the most solemn yet festive of all the sabbats. Many are visibly moved in renewing the friendships and loves that death has curtailed. It is a time of communion, of introspection, of learning, as well as a time for delight. Some traditions urge the participants in the Samhain rite to take a moment to say farewell to those who have passed from life in the preceding year. Others may welcome the spirits of ancestors, teachers, and loved ones who have passed on many years prior. This may be particularly true of those who follow a family tradition or who have strong ties to cultural ancestry. Hereditaries often believe that the grandmothers and grandfathers of previous generations are always near to guide them through their lives of growth and development. Many tribal and specific culture-based traditions look to the spirits of departed heroes and ancestors to strengthen them in their own daily trials.

For many, this sabbat also marks the changing of the year. It is the time when all the plant life returns to the earth for its winter slumber. The first evidence is seen as the leaves change to reds, browns, and golds, and fall from their perches to the soil below.

Toward the end of December arrives the Winter Solstice and the time for the Yule celebration. The Winter Solstice marks the shortest day of the year. This is the time when life retreats from the earth, when all is still and bleak within the cold grip of winter. It is the time when the Lord of the Underworld, the God of Death is most apparent. This is the Pagan celebration of the Dark Lord.

But it is also a celebration of the life that is born in the womb of death. For though the Sun shines most briefly at this time, and winter is most apparent, from this time forward it will increase its light day by day. For this reason, while the Dark Lord is honored at the Yule celebration, it is also the festival of the birth of the Young Lord—the birth of the Sun. As the young God grows older, so will his symbol, the Sun, shine down more brightly and warmly each day.

Many of the traditional Christmas symbols originated in Pagan Yule festivities, and are still used by Pagans throughout the world. A Yule tree is often chosen and decorated amidst dancing and song in honor of the God. In this way, Pagans rejoice in his birth and encourage his continued growth. An evergreen tree is chosen as the ritual tree, not only as the symbol of the God, but as a reminder that life is ever-constant and ever-renewed. The Yule log (usually of oak, a wood sacred to the Dark Lord) is often burned in a ritual fire. In some groups, the Yule celebration, marking the end of the calendar year, is an opportunity to remember the gifts received throughout the year, and an opportunity to remember the bounty of the Goddess as well as the God by honoring each Moon that rose throughout the passing year. It is also a time to show appreciation for the love, support, companionship, and friendship of those with whom we share our daily lives. It is a time for the making and giving of Yule gifts as tokens of love.

Candlemas, Imbolc, Oimelc, or the Festival of Light is the next sabbat to grace the Pagan year. While the world is still in the icy grip of winter, this sabbat is celebrated as a time to remember the warmth of the Sun and to give reverence to the young Sun God as he grows to fullness. It is a time of hope, of looking forward. Although the cold has not yet released the earth to spring, we know that as surely as day follows night, the Sun God will return in all his glory, and, with the Goddess, will bring renewed life to the land.

One of the traditional customs at this time is to light candles to the honor of the young God, to encourage his growth and returning. Another is the passing of the touch-stone. A piece of lapis lazuli is placed in a dish of water and passed around the circle. Each participant, in turn, touches his or her hand to the stone, and then to the "third eye." This may arouse clairvoyance in some. Others may feel a blending of the essence of the God and Goddess, and a renewed sense of balance within themselves.

As the cycle of the seasons progresses, the Earth is visited by the Spring Equinox, a time that finds the Pagan people in celebration of the Rites of Spring. As the Sun's presence is more apparent upon the Earth, the first signs of rebirth and renewal are seen. In classical mythology, it is said that this is when Persephone begins her journey back to her mother's side. Demeter, the Goddess of the Earth, in anticipation of her daughter's return, begins to tend to the earth once again. Trees begin to cover themselves with green splendor, grass sprouts up through the barren soil, and birds and creatures rejoice in the warm Sun. It is said that the birds were the first to be aware of the returning Goddess, and herald her coming with their sweet songs in spring.

One of the traditions of Spring Equinox is the baking of a silver coin in sweet bread. The bread is shared by all the Pagan celebrants, and the one who receives the coin is considered especially blessed. He or she will choose a partner, and together they will lead the celebration with a night of games, dance, and song. As the celebration comes to a close, the lady of the Spring Couple will be given a gift of flowers, and both the Spring Lady and Spring Lord will go home with the favor of the God and Goddess.

Some of the other traditions observed at the Spring Equinox are the cutting of the apple, and the blessing of plants. An apple is taken and cut crosswise in honor of Persephone, exposing the seeds laid out in the form of a pentagram. The seeds are removed and blessed, and planted by the next full Moon. In this time of growth and renewal, many bring a young plant to the rites and ask the blessing of the Deities for its healthy continued growth. After the rites, the plants are carried home and nurtured to fullness, now all the more special for the blessing bestowed upon them at the celebration.

May Eve heralds Beltane. Of all the Pagan sabbats, perhaps it is this one that has survived most universally in its original form. The Cauldron and the Maypole (female and male symbols of fertility) are traditionally associated with Beltane. The crowning of a May Queen is another common traditional observance, one that is still practiced among Pagan and non-Pagan May Day revelers alike. The May Day celebration has continued throughout many countries with the traditional Maypole dance. This is essentially a fertility rite. And many non-Pagan people still enjoy the dance who may not think of it in terms of its original purpose.

Often, the Pagan celebrations would last until dawn. As the weary revelers wound their way home, there was another tradition often practiced by the young maidens—they would wash their faces with the water of the first dew of May. This would ensure that they would grow toward fullness and fertility even as the fields of the earth grew to ripeness.

As the Sun reaches its fullest glory, the Summer Solstice arrives, celebrated with the sabbat known as Midsummer. While the Sun is in its greatest splendor, it is a time to give honor to the God, who is at the height of his stature. This is also the time of the Dyad Moon. The fruits of creation are apparent all about us, and the fertility of the Divine Couple is also celebrated in their sacred union.

One of the practices that survives from times past is the making of the love wreath. From ribbons and summer flowers, wreaths are constructed and exchanged by friends as a token of their mutual esteem. Such wreaths grace many homes to this day.

Lammas or Lughnasad is harvest time. On July 31, the Pagan people celebrate their bounty as the year's harvest is gathered. Appropriate to the reaping of the grain, this festival is also known as the Feast of Bread. Baking of bread is a common act of reverence. At this time, the first harvest of the grain is taken, and the bread is the first food of the harvest.

Another harvest-tide observance is the making of corn dollies. Along many a farm route, these quaint figures might be seen for sale. The making of the corn dolly, however, was a ritual act for the Pagan people. From the first harvested corn, the husks are fashioned into a doll figure. The kernels are then removed from the cob and placed into a vessel of water. This vessel is placed so that the Moon will shine its light upon it from waxing to full. The corn doll is then suspended on the inside of the front door of the house, while the vessel of corn is given a place of honor in the home. This is believed to protect the household and ensure good fortune throughout the year. At the time of the following year's harvest, the corn dolls are burned and the corn kernels are buried in the fields, returning the seed to the earth.

There are many customs surviving from the Lammas celebration. Whether of Pagan belief or not, the bounty of the fields and the fruits of the season's labors remain important to those who till the soil. A plentiful harvest is reason enough to celebrate, no matter what name people give their deities.

Finally, as the Pagan year comes full circle, the Autumn Equinox occurs. The stores are full from the harvest, and the labors of the field are at an end.

Stillness and barrenness begins to descend upon the once green fields in this time of transition. Just as the leaves adorn themselves with their coats of many colors, all the earth is changing. It is a time for preparation. Winter is not far away, and all people must make themselves ready for the first snow.

In mythological lore, it is said that the Young Lord has grown to fullness through the year, and warmed the Earth as the growing Sun. Now, in his maturity, he turns to other pursuits, and to the creatures of the woods. We will soon recognize the God as Lord of the Hunt. The Earth Mother retires from her season of bounty, and seeks repose through the winter, so that her tasks of rebirth can begin when the season of rest is over.

This is a time of thanksgiving, and of reverence. We remember the gifts received through the fertility of the Earth, and honor the God and Goddess who bring devastation and fruitfulness in equal measure. The Pagans believe that all that dies will be reborn, that death is a necessary step in the natural cycle, and is inseparable from birth and renewal. Just as death is a necessary end to life, it is through death that the seed of life renewed is made possible.

Having reviewed both the Esbat and Sabbat celebrations, there is one point that is interesting to note. While there are many Pagan and Wiccan practices that retain a matriarchal slant to their beliefs, the celebrations of the Sabbats are solar in nature. The Sun is often considered a male or God symbol. Conversely, the Christian religion (normally seen as dominated by the masculine) takes its year of festival from the Moon, a female or Goddess symbol. Easter, which determines most of the other Christian feasts, occurs on the first Sunday after the first Full Moon following March 21.

So turns the wheel of the Pagan year, ever onward. Marking endings, new beginnings, life, birth, death, and renewal—ever constant, yet ever renewed as time hurries on. Each year brings new celebrations, and new reasons to celebrate. And as the changes in the natural cycles are marked by ritual and revelry, the promise of rebirths to come is seen in the celebration of the present.

## Chapter Exercises
Regarding the traditional observances of the seasonal changes marked by each sabbat, what might you do as a simple act of devotion to celebrate each. Do not think in terms of a full scale ritual, but a simple prayer, a personal gesture, a token from the heart.

## Additional Suggested Reading
*Encyclopedia of White Magic: A Seasonal Guide* by Paddy Slade

*Ancient Ways: Reclaiming Pagan Traditions* by Pauline Campanelli

# Chapter Seven

# *The Working Tools*

Since the earliest times, there have been certain instruments of the craeft that have served as aids in worship and magickal rites. Although some working tools are in wider use than others, and there are different opinions regarding the importance of one over the other, many have survived the passage of time and are in active ritual use today.

There are some who believe in hand crafting their own ritual tools from consecrated raw materials. Much can be said in support of this view. The ritual tools are for personal use, and of a very personal nature. When a person fashions a tool by hand, it is embued with that person's own energies. As an extension of its creator, such a tool can be very effective when used in a ritual.

Relatively few people, however, have the skill or knowledge to fashion their own tools. Raw materials and facilities are not commonplace, especially in regard to metal tools that require forging or casting of molten ore. The obvious alternative is to purchase the tools.

There are two basic guidelines that are commonly observed in purchasing tools for ritual use. They are conflicting in nature, and it is a matter of personal belief and training to choose which path to follow. There are some who believe that a tool should be purchased new. That which has been newly manufactured is virgin enough to absorb the energies of the one who uses it, so that it may truly become an extension of its owner. Others are of the opinion that ritual tools should be purchased at a flea market, antique store, or an estate sale. Buying from the "old" sources, it is thought, may bring the seeker to a piece that has absorbed enough energies over the years to have a life and power of its own to augment that of its owner. Perhaps a piece may be found that was actually used in days past as an altar tool.

It should be clarified that while many choose a tool that seems to exhibit a life and energy of its own, the power is not truly lodged in the tool—the strength originates from the owner. The tool simply serves to concentrate and direct the energy raised by its user. Visions are brought to mind of the magician's wand creating havoc in the hands of the unlearned apprentice. So far, I personally have not seen a tool that's worth one whit without its master or mistress. As impressive as they may be by look or feel, without the right wielder, a tool is hardly functional, and only marginally "magickal."

Regardless of the opinion any individual might hold concerning the purchase of the working tools, however, there are some universally held beliefs governing the circumstance of their purchase. There must be a positive feeling surrounding any tool that is to be obtained for ritual use. Ideally, the piece will seem to choose the buyer as much as the buyer chooses it. This may mean that the piece presents itself in some strange or unusual manner just as the user is looking for that type of tool. It may mean that it is received as a gift from someone dear at exactly the appropriate time. It may appear in a meditation or dream, or one may just "know" that a certain tool was destined for them. If there is uncertainty about the feeling of a particular piece, it may be best to forget about it for a time and return to it later. If it is truly destined to be yours, it will still be there when next you visit. Also, never haggle over the price of a ritual piece. This is something that will be dedicated to the God and Goddess, and to bargain over it dishonors them and cheapens its worth. And obviously, any tool obtained for ritual use must be gotten fairly, honestly, and in a positive manner.

Finally, consecrate the ritual piece before putting it into use. Essentially, this means dedicating it to the God and Goddess and asking their blessing for its proper and effective use. In a group or coven situation, the High Priest and High Priestess are generally quite willing to consecrate newly acquired ritual pieces. Solitary consecrations may be as elaborate as full ritual working, or as simple as sincerely asking the blessing of the Deities on your newly obtained ritual tool. Because they become a very personal part of one's ritual work, it is imperative that the practitioner feel good about the tool from its creation or acquisition through its consecration and use. If there are working members of the Priesthood that one feels especially positive about, it is perfectly acceptable to have them consecrate such a personal item as a working tool. However, it is also possible and equally acceptable to consecrate one's own ritual pieces.

## A Simple Consecration Ritual

*Rub salt on the tool and say:*
"I consecrate thee with Earth. May this (tool) be endowed with all the virtues of Earth, and the blessings of the element of Earth be multiplied with its every use."

*Then pass the tool through burning incense, symbolizing Air, with the words:*
"I consecrate thee with Air. May this (tool) be endowed with all the virtues of Air, and the blessings of the element of Air be multiplied with its every use."

*Now pass the tool through a flame, dedicating it to Fire, and say:*
"I consecrate thee with Fire. May this (tool) be endowed with all the virtues of Fire, and the blessings of Fire be multiplied with its every use."

*Next, sprinkle water on the tool and say:*
"I consecrate thee with Water. May this (tool) be endowed with all the virtues of Water, and the blessings of Water be multiplied with its every use."

*Finally, hold the piece aloft in offering to the God and Goddess, saying:*
"Lord and Lady hear me. I offer this (tool) for your blessing. May it ever serve me in earnest, and thee in honor. So Mote It Be!"

Now that the "ground rules" for the acquisition of ritual tools have been set, and a consecration ritual described, the type of working tools to be obtained should be considered. There are many different types of tools employed in ritual use, some in combination with others, some in an alternative capacity. As with many of the practices of Paganism, this is generally a matter of training, tradition, and personal preference. The following are some of the tools that may be employed in ritual work, along with their purpose.

## The Wand

The wand may be made from a number of different woods (crystal wands are a more recent alternative). *The Key of Solomon the King*, an important reference work for ceremonialists, indicates the hazel tree as the best source for the wand. Other preferred materials

*Wands*

include willow, rowan, elder, oak, or any of the various other "sacred" woods of different Pagan and magickal traditions. According to tradition and use, the wand may have different methods of construction and finished appearance. It may be raw wood, colored black and tipped in silver, or painted red and yellow. It may be inscribed with any number of magickal symbols, set with stones or crystal, or adorned with feathers, shells, or other materials. Those of the old religion who employ a wand use it to direct energies raised within a rite to a specific purpose, and for invoking and banishing elemental spirits. Ceremonial magicians may dedicate the wand to the element of fire, and use it in rites of a fiery nature, and for the invocation and banishment of fire spirits.

## The Staff

The staff can be used to mark out the ritual ground in outdoor rites, for pounding on the earth to attract spirits, or (with the inset of a stone) as a power conduit. For example, set with a moonstone, the staff might be used to draw power from the Moon through the staff and into the one who

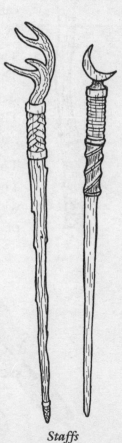

*Staffs*

*Stang*

wields it. The staff is primarily a tool of the ceremonial magician. Those in Pagan circles who employ the staff often do so for much more mundane purposes. They may use it to beat out the rhythm for a ritual dance, or simply as a walking stick. Traditionally, the staff is constructed of elderwood, cane, or rosewood, though many may be seen of birch, maple, and oak.

### The Stang
The stang is a forked version of the staff, constructed of rowan wood. This is used to strike the rhythm in ritual chants and dances.

### The Athame
The athame, a black-hilted knife, is in wide use throughout many traditions of Paganism or Wicca, as well as in

*Athames*

ceremonial rites. It is used is used to trace pentacles for invoking and banishing rites, in salutes to the Deities, and in directing energies to a predetermined purpose. Ceremonial magicians use it as a magickal weapon to subdue and control rebellious spirits. Like the staff, it can also be used to symbolically cut a sacred space in which to conduct ritual work.

## The Boline
The boline or white-hilted knife is a practical working blade. Where the athame is generally employed as a magickal instrument, the boline is more utilitarian. It may be used for cutting runic symbols in magickal candles, for harvesting needed herbs, or for any other cutting or carving required in preparation for ritual or magickal work. There are some who assert that this blade should only be used within the con-fines of the ritual circle, though oth-

*Boline*

ers suggest that it may be difficult to cull herbs from any place other than where they actually grow. There are other less common blades that may be used for the same purposes as the Boline. They include the sickle, the scintar, the burin, and the short lance. Though similar in application, these can be distinguished by their different shapes.

*Swords*

## The Sword

The sword is a symbol of authority. In some covens, the sword is passed between High Priest and High Priestess at different times of the year as the leadership of the group changes hands. Beltane (May 1st) is the time for the reign of the Goddess, and the Priestess assumes leadership of the coven. When Hallowmas (October 31) comes around, the God reigns, and the Priest, as his earthly representative, holds the sword. Like the athame, the sword may be used to mark the sacred ground, and is sometimes used in place of an athame by the Priest during the reign of the God.

## The Dagger

The dagger is used in ceremonial rites to symbolize the element of air, in the performance of rituals of an airy nature, and for invoking and banishing spirits of the air.

## The Cup

The cup or chalice is a symbol of water and of the Goddess. It is most commonly used as a receptacle for the ritual wine.

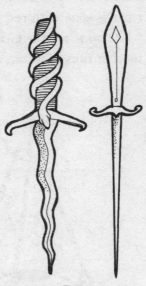

*Daggers*

*Cups*

However, some traditions employ two chalices in their rituals—one with red wine for the God, and one with white wine for the Goddess. In ceremonial circles, it is used in rites of water, and to call the water spirits.

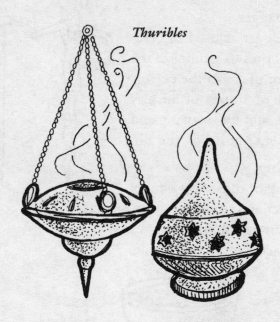

*Thuribles*

## The Thurible

The thurible or censer is placed on the altar as a symbol of air. Incense is burned in the thurible during rituals. Various scents may be used to honor the Deities or to reflect the time of year, or the celebration of a particular type of rite, or to cleanse the circle with the element of air, and to give honor to its elemental realm.

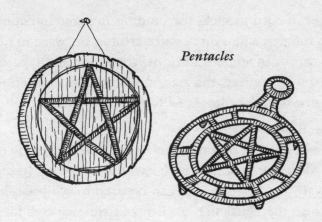

*Pentacles*

## The Pentacle

The pentacle is a symbol of earth. Ceremonialists use it for earth rites and to call on the earth spirits. In Pagan circles, it may be used to cast the circle by rolling the disc around its circumference, or as a plate for ritual cakes, eaten as a reminder that the grain originates from the earth. Generally, the pentacle is fashioned of a copper disc with a pentagram carved on its face. However, in the past, pentacles were sometimes formed of wax.

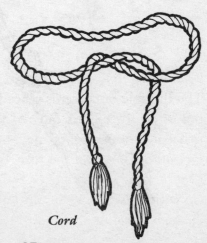

## The Cord

The cord is also known as the girdle, the cingulum, or the cable tow. This may be used in some

*Cord*

types of cord magick, for binding in some initiation ceremonies, and is often worn around the waist in ritual work. In some traditions, the color and type of cord worn reflects the station of the person wearing it—the degree or level of Priesthood attained.

## The Besom

The besom is a broom which is traditionally made of six different woods: birch, willow, broom, hazel, rowan, and hawthorn. It can be used to symbolically cleanse the ritual site, and in old times was ridden

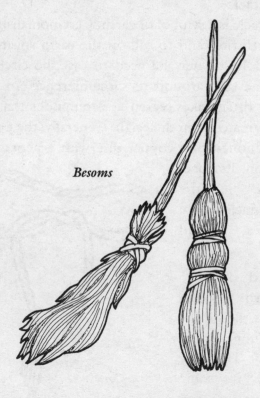

*Besoms*

hobby-horse style through the fields while the rider jumped to show the crops how high to grow in a rite of sympathetic magick. This use of the besom may be what has given rise to the vision of witches riding through the night astride their brooms. Those who jumped the highest must have made a silhouette against the moon that was not unlike the decorative placards that are common when Halloween approaches.

*Scourge*

## The Scourge

The scourge is used for ritual purification in some traditions. There have been stories of its use as a tool of punishment for those who have wronged or betrayed their coven, but this is not a common use. Many feel that if an offense is grave enough to warrant flogging, then it must certainly be worthy of banishment from the group.

## The Cauldron

The cauldron is a female symbol. Traditionally it is made of cast iron, and has three legs reflecting the Maiden, Mother, and Crone aspects of the Goddess. Modern uses have included using it as a safe place in

*Cauldrons*

which to build a ritual fire for indoor rituals. In old times, it was used as a stewing pot for the preparation of the sabbat feasts.

**The Book of Shadows**

The Book of Shadows is a book of rituals. It may also be known as the Red Book, the Grimoire, the Black Book, or the Witch's Workbook. It may contain sabbat rites, spells, rituals, herbal remedies, and folk lore.

During the persecution of Pagans, ritual tools were certain physical evidence against the accused. Accordingly, there were strict precautions to be taken in regard to working tools. Some traditions still open their Book of Shadows with the following passage that is reflective of those dangerous times:

**Book of Shadows**

*To avoid discovery, let the working tools be as ordinary things that any may have in their houses. Let the pentacles be of wax so that they may be broken at once or melted. Have no sword unless your rank allows you one. Have no names or signs on anything. Write the names or signs in ink immediately before consecrating them, and wash it off immediately afterwards. Do not engrave them lest they cause discovery. Let the color of the hilts tell which is which.*

*Keep a book in your own hand of write. Let brothers and sisters copy what they will, but never let the book out of your hands, and never keep the writings of another. For if it be in their hand of write, they may be taken and engrained. Let each guard his own writings, and destroy them whenever danger threatens. Learn as much as you can by heart, and when the danger is past, re-write your book an it be safe. For this reason, if any die, destroy their book an they have not been able to. For an it be found, 'tis clear proof against them. And our oppressors know well, ye may not be a witch alone.*

This sentiment, originally shared by a priestess from a tradition other than my own, captures the air of fear and the need for caution that pervaded the "burning times." Of course, it is appropriate that it has been taken as a common opening of the Grimoire within a coven, for it addresses the dangers of unity. It does not, however, speak to the village wise woman, the hermit Pagan who dwells deep within the woods and lives in the company of the beasts, or even many modern-day Pagans, who worship the God and Goddess in private, and practice their art in solitude. Yet, one cannot help but feel that while it may not be true that "Ye may not be a witch alone," Pagans throughout the world who follow the ways of the old religion, even those who choose to enter into their rites a lone practitioner, are never truly alone. They share their ways with so many others of a common heart.

## Chapter Exercises

Take a walk in the woods, the mountains, on the seashore, or even in the local park. Open your mind, and let yourself be drawn to that special item that will become a special working tool for you. You may end up with a fallen branch that will become a wand or a staff. You may find a discarded bit of metal that will be the blade of an athame, or a bit of lost deer horn that will become its hilt. It may be a special stone that draws your eye. Take your treasure home with you and meditate with it. Let you and it mutually discover your destiny together. Even if you find that what you have found is simply a wonderful bit of nature with which to meditate, this is as valuable a tool for you as one of the more traditional working tools might be for another. Cherish it.

## Additional Suggested Reading

While many of the other suggested texts include sections concerning tools used in various rituals, and in different traditions, this is a very personal venture, and I am reluctant to suggest any material specifically directed toward the construction or acquisition of ritual equipment. However, for those who might feel slighted if this chapter excludes additional material, here are some fun books for you to peruse:

*The Witches Broomstick Manual* by Rev. Yaj Nomolos

*The Witch's Handbook* by Malcolm Bird

# Chapter Eight

## The Temple
## and the Altar

The ritual place of the Pagan people may take on different characteristics. Since the practice of the old religion is closely tied to the cycles of nature, many prefer to conduct their rituals outside, close to the elements. Some, however, erect their temples indoors. While some practice exclusively one way or the other, others change their ritual site in accordance with their circumstances, whether because the weather is harsh, or there is a need for privacy, or the usual site is temporarily unavailable, etc. Once again, it is largely a matter of personal choice.

An indoor Pagan temple is a place that has been dedicated to the honor of the God and Goddess, and should be maintained accordingly. Even in homes that do not otherwise reflect a great deal of housekeeping, the temple should be kept as immaculate as possible. The temple should be thoroughly scrubbed from top to bottom at least once a month, and the altar tools cleaned and shined. This full cleansing, in addition to being done as a regular practice, is also done prior to every Sabbat ritual. It is generally the responsibility of the High Priestess to see that this is done.

In some traditions, my own included, floors are scrubbed in the old way—on hands and knees, very carefully, and very thoroughly. Often, some hyssop is boiled down to add to the cleaning pail to aid in cleansing the "non-physical" grime. This is done by taking about a quarter to a half ounce of the herb, and bringing it to a boil over a flame (or on top of the stove!). When it boils, remove it from the heat or turn down the stove and let it simmer until the water has drawn enough of the herb to appear like tea. Strain the solution. Many like to offer the cleansing water to the Deities before setting it to its purpose. One of the simpler blessings would be to raise the solution in offering with the words, "Herbs of the earth, beloved of the Sun, tended by the Stars, kissed by the Moon, held by the Goddess, given by the God, Blessed Be!" Then you are ready to cleanse the space, removing all physical and non-physical distractions.

Prior to every ritual, the temple should be well swept. Some traditions use a ritual sweeping to cleanse the sanctuary of any negativity, ill feeling, or conflicting energies. When this is done, it should be largely a ritual act, not a physical need!

Exactly how the temple space is set up is largely a matter of individual taste, personal choice, and chosen tradition. Some may paint circles or pentagrams on the floor, walls, or ceilings. The room may be decorated with murals reflecting mythology, ritual practices, or traditional beliefs. The walls might be hung with paintings of special significance, or the room adorned with statues to the honor of the God and Goddess. If one is so inclined, the temple may be filled with plants, or perhaps contain an aquarium. The Pagan rites are celebrations of life and love, and to fill the temple with life can only serve to reinforce the Pagan rituals that occur. Whatever tone the temple takes, it must be remembered that the temple is a consecrated sanctuary and a doorway to the God and Goddess. It should be treated reverently.

A word of caution—be discriminating about who is allowed to set foot in your consecrated space! Its nature and its purpose should be respected by all who enter into it. Temples become very sensitive to the vibrations and energies to which they are exposed. They can absorb the negative as easily as the positive. So, by all means, do not profane your sanctuary by exposing it to those who would not treat it with due respect. Should there be any unintentional defiling of your sacred space, be quick to cleanse it of the negative energies and restore its sanctity.

Above all, the temple is not merely an "extra room" in your house, and should never be used as a convenient sleeping or dining area. This warning is not meant to preclude the traditional ritual sharing of cakes and ale as practiced by many traditions. Food and drink are common elements of the celebration, and ritual wine or shared festivities are a welcome activity within the sacred space, but if the sustenance is not taken in honor of the Old Ones or in the spirit of Pagan love, it is a mundane activity, and out of place in a consecrated space.

When Pagans gather for a Sabbat or other ritual celebration, late hours may demand that they stay the night, but the temple is no place for a slumber party! While Paganism is a celebration of life, and Paganism welcomes shared festivities, the temple must retain its sacred demeanor. Whatever takes place within its walls should be free of mundane or frivolous influences. Be ever mindful that this is a place that has been sanctified, and should be treated reverently.

Of course, not everyone is in a position to keep a separate temple room. Many Pagans must set up their altars anew each time they need them—on a coffee table in the living room, a dresser in the bedroom, or at the kitchen table. The sanctification of this temporary working space is just as important, however. All the observances of cleanliness and reverence still apply. It takes but a few moments to clear away a stack of books and magazines, to clean up the dinner dishes, or to make the bed. Massive clutter is simply not conducive to good ritual work. Aside from being an indication of an apparent lack of proper attitude, clutter can be distracting enough to pull your thoughts away from what you are doing. Rituals should be entered into with clarity. One should be free of the thoughts and pressures of mundane living, and open to know the grace and the glory of the Pagan Deities.

For outdoor ritual work, the space is carefully chosen. Often, an area with Pagan roots is chosen, such as an area with a known history of Pagan worshippers in the past. Or it may be chosen by the feeling it inspires. Perhaps a covener has some land that he or she wishes to dedicate to the God and Goddess, or a friend offers the use of some property as a gesture of love and kindness. I know of one group that got permission from their local government to hold their rituals in a public park.

Proper care of the ritual site is no less important outdoors than it is in an indoor temple. The place should be kept free of rubbish and debris, and allowed to retain its natural beauty. One of the responsibilities of Pagans practicing a nature religion in nature's own setting is to preserve and protect the land. The outdoor site is nature's gift, and one needn't attempt to "improve" on it. Like an indoor space, the outdoor site should be cleaned up when the rite is done. Anything that has been brought to the site should be carried away when you quit the grounds, leaving the space as natural and pure as when you first arrived.

Like the temple, the altar may vary in accordance with tradition and personal preferences. The type of altar may also vary according to the circumstances. For outdoor circles, many prefer a natural altar. This may take the form of a long flat stone laid across a base of two smaller ones, a natural ledge in the side of a cliff, or a tree stump still rooted in the earth.

Some prefer a more natural type of altar for use in indoor rites as well. Other options include obtaining a piece of furniture that has a good "feel" to it. It may be a table, bureau, desk, vanity—almost anything that would serve the function. Many Pagans favor antique pieces for use as their altars. Others feel that their altars should come from the labor of their own hands. Then there are those who construct their altars in accordance with certain Pagan or magickal traditions or special significations. Such a case is the

**Stone Altar**

**Double Cube Altar**     **Stump Altar**

double cube altar of ceremonial magicians which signifies the maxim "As above, so below."

While the type of altar may vary with different traditions and personal preferences, there are some observances that are more universal. Upon erecting a new altar and preparing it for use, many of the same considerations are taken as with the temple space. The altar itself is cleansed, possibly using the same solution of hyssop as used in the temple.

On the altar will be the ritual tools. Although the ritual pieces used and the manner in which they are set will vary from one altar to the next, there are certain general observances that are shared by many traditions. There is usually a ritual cup or chalice placed on the altar, and candles or lamps for illumination. Often a representation of the Deity will be present on the altar. Sometimes this is a statue depicting the God or Goddess, or a symbol considered sacred to them.

Also in evidence is usually some sort of representation of the elements of earth, air, fire, and water—the basic elements of all creation. Possible ways to represent the four elements are as follows:

**Earth**
A dish of loam or salt; a copper disc inscribed with a pentagram or other symbol of earth.

**Air**
A censer with incense that burns throughout the rites; a wand or sword (depending on tradition); feathers; a bell.

### Fire
A dish of oil with floating wick; a candle (usually red); a sword or knife dedicated to the element of fire; a wand (as above: different traditions may use opposite symbols for fire and air).

### Water
A cup or bowl filled with water (some add sea salt to the water to emulate the natural water of the Earth's oceans); seashells; driftwood; seaweed (such as a dish of kelp).

Sometimes combining elemental symbols is convenient for those with limited resources or who are just setting up their altars. In this case, the censer can be used to represent both fire and air. Salt can be added to the water dish to symbolize earth as well as water. Other optional items on the altar can include:

### The Source Candle
Usually black, it represents the light that shines forth from the void. It symbolizes the spark of life that stands behind even the God and Goddess. Within the doctrines of many traditions, it is held that all Gods are one God, all Goddesses are one Goddess, and they emerge from a single source that is the beginning of all creation. The Source Candle is a symbol of that oneness.

### The Illumination Candle (or Working Candle)
The color is taken from the traditional colors associated with each of the thirteen Moons of the years.

The flame represents the light of the Sun, while the candle itself symbolizes the Moon's reflection of the light. Both Sun and Moon, or male and female principles, are represented in this way. The purpose of the illumination candle, aside from its symbolism, is simply to provide light.

## God and Goddess Candle

Those who follow traditions that believe in a balance between male and female may have a candle on their altars for both the God and the Goddess. These may be gold and silver, white and black, red and green, or whatever other colors are deemed fitting and proper. This may be determined by tradition, personal taste, or the time of year.

## The Two Pillars

These are two candles (usually black and white) used to represent the universal male and female, or active and passive principles. Some leave these lights burning at all times to symbolize the ever-present nature of these two universal forces. Although these components are more at home on the altar of the ceremonial magician, there is often a sharing of practices between Pagans and other related systems.

## The Libation Dish

Many Pagans believe in offering back to the Deities the gifts given by them to Humanity. Ritual wine and cakes are first offered in this way before being shared by those within the rite. When a ritual takes place outdoors, the wine is often poured directly to the earth in offering. Indoors, however, the offering is placed in the libation dish and poured to the earth when the rite has ended.

## The Eternal Light

A candle, gas lamp, or lantern which is kept on a small altar to the side of the main one, or suspended from the wall or ceiling. This light is kept burning all the time as a symbol and a gesture of respect to the force of life that permeates the universe (much like the source candle).

## The Seasonal Candle

Utilized in much the same manner as the Eternal Light, this is a candle that is constantly kept burning, but is reflective of the current season. Some groups use a green candle through the spring and summer months, and change to red for the autumn and winter. Others may change the color four times during the year, once for each of the seasons.

## Flowers

There may be fresh flowers set upon the altar out of respect to the God and Goddess, and to add to the good feeling of the rituals to be undertaken.

## The Altar Veil

A cloth is sometimes used to veil the altar when it is not in use. This is primarily a gesture of respect. Similarly, some may wrap and put away their altar tools when not in use.

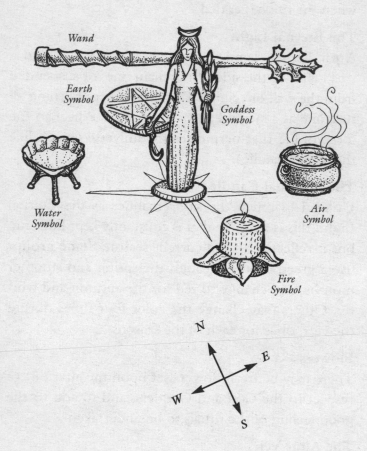

Wand

Earth
Symbol

Goddess
Symbol

Water
Symbol

Air
Symbol

Fire
Symbol

N

E

W

S

*This is a basic arrangement used by one matriarchal group.
For illumination, they place a candle at each of the cardinal
points of the temple.*

116

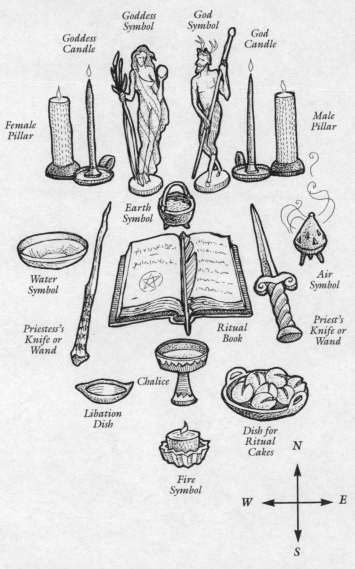

Goddess
Symbol

God
Symbol

Goddess
Candle

God
Candle

Female
Pillar

Male
Pillar

Earth
Symbol

Air
Symbol

Water
Symbol

Priestess's
Knife or
Wand

Ritual
Book

Priest's
Knife or
Wand

Chalice

Libation
Dish

Dish for
Ritual
Cakes

N

W — E

Fire
Symbol

S

*This is an altar setup that might be employed by those who
follow a more balanced tradition of Paganism.*

# Chapter Nine

## *The Ritual*

On a very basic level, the ritual is a practical working procedure that can be used for the realization of an almost unlimited range of intentions. For instance, it can be employed as a means of worship, a method of energy raising for use in healing or other magickal purposes, or a rite of celebration to mark a certain milestone in one's life.

The effective working of a ritual will often be the result of many factors. Instinct and training will both play their parts. Sincerity is a key factor. Practice and solid experience, however, are paramount to safe and successful ritual work.

Ideally, ritual is learned over a period of time, initially by observation and limited participation, then by taking an active role under the guidance of someone of wider knowledge and experience, and finally by working without supervision to develop practical experience of one's own. Training should be readily and constantly available so that ritual work is based on sound knowledge. The stories recounted about those who step into ritual work without some sound understanding as to what they're doing and why they are doing it are cautionary, and far more numerous than they should be.

Unfortunately, although adequate training is, in my own view, the best possible foundation for safe and effective ritual work, I am reminded that this is something that is not always readily available. For many who enter onto a Pagan path, the first steps are taken through reading books and trying "this and that" to see if it is, in fact, the right direction for them. The reading list at the end of this chapter includes some volumes that could prove very helpful for those entering into ritual work on their own, without the benefit of an experienced guide. Some include actual solitary rituals. Others, while designed for group working, will illustrate how a rite may be put together, and may even be easily adapted for solitary practice.

At the least, the ritual is a tool and should be treated as such. It should be remembered, though, that while a power saw in the hands of a skilled carpenter may be an asset to his trade, the same device in the hands of a child might produce little more that severed fingers. The intention here is not to discourage ritual work, for effective working can yield incredible benefits. However, it is important to emphasize that training and knowledge are the foundation on which safe and successful ritual work is built.

## Key Elements of Ritual Work

Although there are different ways of working, certain key elements are apparent in most ritual work. The following is an outline of a sample format that can be adapted to many different Pagan traditions.

- Establishing Intention
- Preparing the Ritual
- Preparing the Temple
- Casting the Circle
- Calling the Quarters
- Calling the Deities
- Fulfillment of Purpose
- Thanksgiving and Farewell
- Closing the Circle

These individual components will be delineated one by one. It may be helpful upon reading through the actual ritual work included to refer back to these steps to see how they are applied in the actual circle. Following the discussion on ritual construction, I will give examples to illustrate the application of these principles for further clarification.

As with most things, there is more than one road that leads to the same destination. For each of the components in the listed ritual outline, several possible methods will be listed. It is also important to note the differences between different ways of working, and to repeat that these differences are only a reflection of personal tradition, preference, and training. Here, then, is the basic format and the primary elements of a ritual.

## Establishing Intention

Every rite must have a purpose. Whether it is a worship circle, healing rite, celebration of the seasons, or a ritual for some special goal, the reason for the rite should be clearly defined before the work is undertaken.

## Preparing the Ritual

With the intention well defined, the next step is to decide how it is to be accomplished. Those who feel comfortable working astrologically may want to choose the ideal day and hour to conduct their rites according to planetary influence. Appropriate planetary colors may be chosen for candles, altar cloths, or robes. Traditional ritual passages may be chosen for invocations, petition, thanksgiving, or whatever else might be aligned with the purpose of the rite. Chants, songs, or dances may be selected for energy raising or celebration. Many people prefer to write out a general outline or "check list" of their planned ritual.

## Preparing the Temple

The temple is cleaned in the usual manner in preparation for the rites to be done. Any working tools or other necessities are prepared and laid out for use. If they are to be used, wine and cakes are set in the temple. Even if the ritual is to be a meditative one, the proper observances are heeded and due preparation completed. Any clutter is removed from the working area. Everything is readied to create the right atmosphere for the ritual as well as preparing the physical requirements of the rite. Mind and body are also prepared. A ritual bath may be taken as a symbolic cleansing of the practitioner. An appropriate scented oil may be used for anointing. Ritual dress (a robe or other ritual attire) may be donned. A meditation may be entered into to attune the individual with the ritual purpose and ready the mind for the rites ahead.

## Casting the Circle

At this point, all has been made ready for the ritual work. The act of casting the circle creates a place of sanctity in which the ritual is to be performed. There are many ways to accomplish this. A pentacle may be rolled around the circumference of the circle, marking its boundaries. The space may by symbolically "cut" with a sword or athame. The elemental symbols may be carried around the circle to set it apart. The concept of "blue fire" may be used to mark the sacred grounds. This is largely a visualization technique in which blue flame is visualized around the edges of the ritual site, and the space is actually defined by pure intentioned energy. This can be done with or without the aid of a sword, wand, or athame. A staff or wand can be used to trace the perimeter of the circle, or an unbroken line of salt can be used to mark out the ritual space.

## Calling the Quarters

From each of the cardinal directions, the elemental spirits are called and asked to attend the rites and lend their strengths to the ritual being done. Depending on the tradition, these spirits may be known as the guardians, the mighty ones, the watchtowers, and in some systems with more of a hint of the Judeo-Christian influence, the archangels. Some of the names used for these entities are as follows:

| NORTH | EAST | SOUTH | WEST |
|---|---|---|---|
| Farren | Fileet | Flamel | Fanice |
| Boreas | Eurus | Notus | Zephyr |
| Morias | Urias | Arias | Senias |
| Agla | YodHeVauHe | Adonai | Eheieh |
| Auriel | Raphael | Michael | Gabriel |

Some traditions trace pentagrams over each quarter as they welcome the elemental spirits; some may offer salute with their athame; others let their words of welcome suffice.

### Calling the Deities
From the heart with original sentiments, or through the use of traditional calls, the Deities are also welcomed to attend and participate in the Pagan rites.

### Fulfillment of Purpose
Having cast the circle, and called upon the deities for their strength and blessing, it is time to address the purpose for which the rite is being held. This usually includes raising energies to apply to a specific purpose, which may include initiation or dedication rites, magickal workings to benefit those within or outside the group, or a seasonal celebration.

### Thanksgiving and Farewell
With the work of the ritual accomplished, many groups give thanks to the God and Goddess for their attendance and for their help and support in the realization of the ritual goal. Likewise, the elemental spirits are given thanks for their part in the rites. Then they are bid farewell as the time comes to close the circle and end the rite.

### Closing the Circle
There are many ways to close the circle. Often the method chosen depends on how the circle was originally cast. Many choose to "undo" the casting, and

so use the casting method in reverse. For example, if "blue fire" was used to cast the circle, it is visualized fading away as the rite is ended. A besom may be used to ritually "sweep away" the circle. If salt was used to mark out the circle, the solid ring is broken. Alternately, the symbol of the fire element, the fire candle, may be carried around the perimeter of the circle to "burn it out." Another very simple but effective method of closing the rites is for the altar candles to be extinguished with the firm declaration, "This rite has ended."

After the ritual has ended comes the clean-up phase, or reconstructing the temple. Any special tools brought into the temple are removed and put away. If a libation dish has been used, its contents are given to the earth and the dish returned to the altar or put away. If an altar veil is used, it is replaced once the altar is cleaned up and made ready for its next use.

If the ritual is conducted outside, the same observances are kept. The grounds should be restored to their natural state. Any residue from the ritual fire should be cleaned up. Any materials brought to the ritual site should be cleared and carried away. The Pagan people follow a way of respect for the natural order. How they tend to the earth in their ritual workings should reflect this deep sense of honor.

## A Sample Ritual

Whether a rite of reverence for the God and Goddess, a circle of healing or of magick, consecration of a new temple, rite of passage, or celebration of a Pagan festival, there are many simple formats that might be used to accomplish your ritual goals. The following is but one of many possible approaches.

## Preparation

The participants in the ritual may do a personal symbolic cleansing before entering the rite. This may take the form of a ritual bath to which appropriate herbs or scents have been added—perhaps hyssop for its cleansing properties, pine and rose (sacred to the God and Goddess), or cedar for its calming properties. The possibilities are unlimited.

Following the bath, an anointing is done with either an essential oil or with a solution of red wine and salt. Traditionally, the points of anointing are the forehead, heart, the wrists, the area just above the genitals, the knees, and the feet. The following words are used at each point of anointing:

Forehead: "Blessed be my mind. May it be filled with knowledge."

Heart: "Blessed be my heart. May it be filled with love."

Wrists: "Blessed be my life, that I may serve the Lord and Lady."

Genital Area: "Blessed be my nature. May it be fertile and produce beauty."

Knees: "Blessed be my knees. May they kneel at the sacred altar for all time."

Feet: "Blessed be my feet. May they walk the path that has been chosen for me with purpose and in truth."

Next, the circle participants may be asked to gather and sit while the priest leads them in a meditation to set the mood and ready them for the rite that is about to begin. The following is a sample meditation that would be recited by the priest for a New Moon celebration.

Priest: "Relax. Let your eyes softly close. Feel the peace within.

Now, cast your mind's eye to the blackened sky. Most nights we see the Lady's Moon cradled in the clouds. We know that she reflects the golden light of our Lord in her silver splendor. We know that our Gods are with us and we are comforted.

But this night, we see no light. No Moon, crescent or full, graces the darkened heavens. Yet look closely, ever so closely. There amid the darkness appears a twinkle of light. And there another, and yet another.

Let the stars shine as beacons. Let them ever remind us that the light of our Gods can never truly die.

This is a time of endings and new beginnings. Let our faith be constant and renewed. When we feel the darkness in our own lives, let us remember the ever-present stars and be comforted.

Look again at the sky. Choose the brightest,

loveliest star. Reach out and pull it into your own being. Feel it in your heart as a warm and comforting love. Now dedicate it to the honor of the ones we are here to serve."

The circle is now entered. When everyone is welcomed into the circle and situated, the altar candles are lit and the ritual is begun with the blessing of the salt and water.

## Blessing of Salt and Water

Priest: "Blessed salt, symbol of earth—Be new, be holy, be pure."

(The priest draws a pentagram in the salt with ritual blade. He then takes three measures of salt on the blade, and places them in the dish of water.)

"Blessed water, place of birth—Be new, be holy, be pure."

(The priest draws a pentagram in the water and consecrates it.)

## Calling the Quarters

As the priest takes each of the elemental symbols around the circle in turn, the Priestess evokes the elemental spirits by name.

Priestess: "Guardians of the (North, East, South, or West); Spirits of the (Earth, Air, Fire, or Water); we ask your presence here this night. Be you welcomed in peace. Blessed Be!"

All Participants: "Blessed Be!"

## Evocations of the God and Goddess

Priest: "O Lady of the New Moon, of beginnings and forgettings, we are gathered here in your name. Grant us your presence, we pray, in this time and in this season, that we may grow new again in spirit and soul, and thus to honor you more. Be you welcomed in peace. Blessed Be!"

All: "Blessed Be!"

Priestess: "In this time and in this season, the Moon has waned, and starts again on her eternal course. It is a time of darkness, but, also of renewal, and the gathering of great tides. We call on you, O Ancient King, to join our rites if you will. And bless us, that we may renew and strengthen ourselves yet once more. Be you welcomed in peace. Blessed Be!"

All: "Blessed Be!"

## The Wine Blessing

The Priest and Priestess kneel facing each other. The Priestess cradles a chalice of wine in her hands. The Priest holds his ritual blade.

Priest: "The Sun brings forth the beginning."

Priestess: "The Moon holds it in darkness."

Both: "As above, so below."

The Knife is now inserted in cup, symbolizing the male/female union.

Priest: "The knife is to the male..."

Priestess: "As the cup is to the female."

Both: "There is no greater magick in the world
than that of a man and a woman joined in the
bonds of love."

The Priest and Priestess rise. The priest takes the chalice, holds it aloft, and asks the blessing of the God.

Priest: "Great Lord, our lives with all life are one.
By darkest night, or brightest Sun,
Ancient King, on thee we call,
To bring your blessings to creatures, all.
Blessed Be!"

(Wine is shared by all participants.)

**Blessing of the Cakes**
The Priestess offers up ritual cakes to the Goddess.

Priestess: "Lady Mother, as we eat,
Grant your blessings on creations all.
Bless us, that we love all things in nature,
And are one with creatures, great and small.
Blessed Be!"

(Cakes are shared by all within the circle.)

**Dedication to the Virtues**
A thurible and a dish of hyssop are placed in the center of the circle.

Priest: "The New Moon is a time of endings and
of new beginnings. Remember the virtues:

Love, for all beings.

Trust, in your fellow man, in your Gods, and in the laws of nature.

Balance, throughout your life.

Humility, let us live and love as one.

Learning, may it never cease.

Reincarnation. Remember well the promise of the cycle.

Harmony, within yourself, and with the world.

Tolerance, with all who dwell within and without the Pagan circle.

Now, each in turn, place a pinch of herb on the burning coals in offering to your Gods. Ask their help in that virtue you find most lacking within yourself. Then dedicate the next Moon cycle to its realization."

(Each attending the rite places a pinch of hyssop in the censer along with their silent prayer.)

## Pagan Self-Dedication

Priest: "The New Moon is a time of fresh beginnings. All who wish to rededicate themselves to a Pagan way of life and worship, repeat after me:

Lord and Lady, take heed of this, your child.

I do stand humbled before you.

Long have I searched for that which I desire,

To truly know your ways as my own.

I have loved the forests and the fields,

And know that the water of the streams

Is inseparable from the life that flows

Throughout my own body.
When the Sun has set, and the Moon is dark,
Help me to know your presence
In the blackened skies.
Help me to remember
The spark of life
Is ever-present
Reflected in the stars of night.
Let me see the thread of life and love
That runs through all things.
Love is the highest law of nature
And the light that guides me ever closer to thee.
May I ever give worship most high
For I am of thee, and thee of me.
Let me know your ways in all things,
And see the light of wisdom in all ways.
For though the paths of men are many,
All are searching to return to you.
And so do I dedicate myself to thee,
Now and always. So Mote It Be!"

## Farewell to the Quarters

The Priestess salutes each quarter in turn, wishing them farewell.

Priestess: "Guardians of the (North, East, South, or West)...
Spirits of the (Earth, Air, Fire, or Water)...
We thank you for your presence here this night.
As you depart, we bid you hail and farewell."

All: "Hail and farewell!"

**Farewell to the God and Goddess**

Priest: "Gracious Mother, we thank you for your presence this night. We thank you for your love and laughter, for your guidance and wisdom. As you depart, please know that the love of your children remains with you. Hail and farewell!"

All: "Hail and farewell!"

Priestess: "Lord, All-Father, we thank you for being with us this night to share with us your joy and strength. And though you depart from us, we ask that you stay ever close. Hail and farewell!"

All: "Hail and farewell!"

**Ending the Rite**

The altar candles are extinguished as the ritual comes to a close.

Priestess: "This rite is ended!"

Priest: "Let the celebration begin!"

All: "Blessed Be!"

(Often a ritual is followed by feasting, games, and dance—in old times, long into the night.)

This is but one type of ritual, and one way of approaching it. There are many Pagan paths and many ways to enter into ritual work. However, if this type of approach is comfortable to the individual, within it exists a format that may be adapted to any purpose. With an alteration of the meditation used at the onset of the rite, and the replacement of the dedications that occur in the midpoint of the ritual with appropriate practices, this same format may be used for any number of ritual ends.

Upon the review of the original draft of this manuscript, I was wisely reminded that while many of us enjoy the fellowship of Pagan circles in groups, there are many "solitaries"—those who also follow their paths alone. In addition, many of those who are new to the ways of the Old Religion, whether they may ultimately become a part of a working group or not, take their first steps along the path on their own. So the following is the same rite as enacted by the group above, but adapted for use by the solitary practitioner. The purpose, the essence, and even many of the words are the same, but it can be entered into by a lone individual, practicing without a group.

## Blessing of Salt and Water

Solitary: "Blessed salt, symbol of earth—Be new, be holy, be pure."

(Draw a pentagram in the salt with ritual blade, then take three measures of salt on the blade and place them in the dish of water.)

"Blessed water, place of birth—Be new, be holy, be pure."

(Draw a pentagram in the water and consecrate it.)

## Calling the Quarters

Take each of the elemental symbols around the circle in turn, and evoke the corresponding elemental spirits.

> Solitary: "Guardians of the (North, East, South, or West)...
> Spirits of the (Earth, Air, Fire, or Water)...
> I ask your presence here this night. Be you welcomed in peace. Blessed Be!"

## Evocations of the God and Goddess

> Solitary: "O Lady of the New Moon, of beginnings and forgettings...
> I come here in your name. Grant your presence, I pray, in this time and in this season, that I may grow new again in spirit and soul, and thus to honor you more. Be you welcomed in peace. Blessed Be!
> In this time and in this season, the Moon has waned, and starts again on her eternal course. It is a time of darkness, but, also of renewal, and the gathering of great tides. I call on you, O Ancient King, to join these rites if you will. And offer your blessing, that I may be renewed and strengthened yet once more. Be you welcomed in peace. Blessed Be!"

## The Wine Blessing

Hold the wine aloft in offering to the God.

> Solitary: "Great Lord, my life with all life is one.
> By darkest night, or brightest Sun,

> Ancient King, on thee I call,
> To bring your blessings to creatures, all.
> Blessed Be!"

(Drink from the blessed wine.)

## Blessing of the Cakes
Offer up the ritual cakes to the Goddess.

> Solitary: "Lady Mother, as I eat,
> Grant your blessings on creations all.
> Bless me, that I love all things in nature,
> And become one with creatures, great and small.
> Blessed Be!"

(Eat the sacred cake.)

## Dedication to the Virtues
Place a thurible and a dish of hyssop in the center of the circle.

> Solitary: "As the New Moon is a time of endings
>     and of new beginnings, I honor the virtues:
>     Love, for all beings.
>     Trust, in my fellow man, in my Gods, and in
>     the laws of nature.
>     Balance, throughout my life.
>     Humility, may I live and love as one with others.
>     Learning, may it never cease.
>     Reincarnation. I remember well the promise of
>     the cycle.
>     Harmony, within myself, and with the world.
>     Tolerance, with all who dwell within and with-
>     out the Pagan circle."

(Place a pinch of herb on the burning coals in offering to the Gods. Ask their help in that virtue most lacking. Then dedicate the next Moon cycle to its realization.)

**Pagan Self-Dedication**

Solitary: "Lord and Lady, take heed of this, your child.

I do stand humbled before you.

Long have I searched for that which I desire,

To truly know your ways as my own.

I have loved the forests and the fields,

And know that the water of the streams

Is inseparable from the life that flows

Throughout my own body.

When the Sun has set, and the Moon is dark,

Help me to know your presence

In the blackened skies.

Help me to remember

The spark of life

Is ever-present

Reflected in the stars of night.

Let me see the thread of life and love

That runs through all things.

Love is the highest law of nature

And the light that guides me ever closer to thee.

May I ever give worship most high

For I am of thee, and thee of me.

Let me know your ways in all things,

And see the light of wisdom in all ways.

For though the paths of men are many,

> All are searching to return to you.
> And so do I dedicate myself to thee,
> Now and always. So Mote It Be!"

## Farewell to the Quarters

Salute each quarter in turn, wishing them farewell.

> Solitary: "Guardians of the (North, East, South, or West)...
> Spirits of the (Earth, Air, Fire, or Water)...
> Thank you for your presence here this night.
> As you depart, I bid you hail and farewell."

## Farewell to the God and Goddess

> Solitary: "Gracious Mother, thank you for your presence this night. Thank you for your love and laughter, for your guidance and wisdom. As you depart, please know that the love of your children remains with you. Hail and farewell!
> Lord, All-Father, I thank you for being here this night to share your joy and strength. And though you depart from me, I ask that you stay ever close. Hail and farewell!"

## Ending the Rite

Extinguish the altar candles as the ritual comes to a close.

> Solitary: "This rite is ended!"

**Chapter Exercises**

Using the ritual guidelines set out in this chapter (refer back to them as you work!), write a ritual of your own. You may dedicate it to any purpose, use original material, or ritual pieces you have collected and that hold special meaning for you. The only absolute is that the finished piece is workable, and comes from the heart.

**Additional Suggested Reading**

*A Book of Pagan Rituals* edited by Herman Slater
*Magickal Rites from the Crystal Well* by Ed Fitch

# Chapter Ten

# *The Wheel and Pagan Virtues*

O ne of the ways in which Pagan traditions have carried down their
teachings in addition to folklore, rhymes,
and songs is in the use of symbolic
reminders. One of these symbols is the

wheel. This is a stick figure rune of eight spokes radiating from a central point.

A universally applied symbol, the wheel has been used to represent many Pagan precepts, and to note many areas of study and regard. It has been used as a reminder of the eight traditional Pagan sabbats, of the early astrological planetary influences, and of the eight sacred paths of spirituality. Phases of the Sun and Moon may be fitted to the spokes to recall their constant cycles, and to relate their passing to the conditions of humankind. The wheel may be a tool, a sacred symbol of religious doctrine, a calendar, or a guidebook for the seeker of Pagan living.

In times when Pagan belief was considered heresy, it was especially important to have symbolic keys to remember the practices of the old religion without resorting to the recording of Pagan precepts in words that could be used as evidence in a trial. The Wheel, with its many meanings, has served the Pagan community as ritual book, theological text, and almanac. It has enabled many Pagan practices and beliefs to be kept in secret, and so escape the wrath of those who would deny the Pagan people their worship.

One of the doctrines retained in the symbol of the wheel is the list of Pagan virtues. There are eight of them, one for each spoke of the rune. They are love, trust, balance, humility, learning, reincarnation, harmony, and tolerance. Many of the phrases that appear below have been gleaned from the author's own

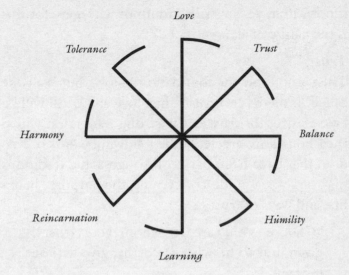

*The Wheel of Virtue*

notes. Some have been passed on through traditional teachings. Others may have been paraphrased from later schools of philosophic thought.

## Love

Love is for the God and the Goddess, and for each other. To know love is to see the common light that runs through all of life, and to truly touch our God and Goddess. Love is to recognize that part within each human spirit that is of the divine realm, and to appreciate its virtue. It is to appreciate the Godlike qualities within ourselves, sometimes as a path to the appreciation of our fellows. It is said that "If you find it not within ye, ye shall find it not without—for this is the nature of all love."

## Trust

Trust is not only the foundation of love, but is a code of life. If there is no trust, then love and truth will be ever elusive, for trust is the strong base upon which their houses are erected. The following words of wisdom that have been passed through some traditions may serve as a guide concerning the purpose, benefits, and ways of trust.

> "Choose with care to whom your trust is given, but to he who is worthy, give without restraint."

> "If ye cannot trust he who would teach, put not thy learning in his charge, but let knowledge be sought elsewhere."

> "There are some things that need be accepted with trust, until time lights the way to understanding."

> "Know well, that what ye distrust shall be inhibited."

## Balance

Balance is sought in a personal as well as a universal sense. The Pagan people seek balance within themselves, within nature, and within the universe, for to lose balance within one's own being is to lose balance with the natural order and with the Deities. Balance is an understanding of the worlds of nature and humanity as reflections of the realm of the Divine, encompassed in the saying "As above, so below." The concept of balance within some traditions of Paganism also encompasses a balance between male and female. Just as male and female principles are imperative in nature for the creation of life, the two work best when they work together in every aspect of living. "For there is no greater power in the world than that of a man and a woman joined in the bonds of love."

## Humility

The virtue of humility is essential for the exercise of all the other virtues. To be open to others and to the ways of the God and Goddess, it is necessary that one not be full of oneself. It is humility that colors our dealings with our fellow beings. It is lack of humility that prevents peace, development, and learning. To truly know humility is to be at home with whatever events come your way, seeing that all circumstances can be turned into learning experiences. It is humility that helps us to see potential in others. The wisest teacher will never rise to a level where he or she is above learning from his or her student. It is humility that reinforces our appreciation of virtue in others, and makes us reluctant to give ourselves over to judgment of another's faults without recognition of the virtues they possess. It is humility that helps to bind Pagans of different paths together, stronger for their acceptance of each others' differences. "Think not that you must extinguish everyone else's candle that your own may cast a light."

## Learning

Learning is a constant endeavor. It is through learning the lessons that the world has to teach that we may come to understand the ways of the Divine. With higher understanding through learning comes the closeness to the divine realm that is desired, and so relentlessly pursued. The more the seeker learns, the greater becomes the need to learn. On a spiritual path, each bit of knowledge attained seems to hold the key to the next level of understanding, and as the level of knowledge increases, so does the vastness of that which is left to attain become more and more visible. For those who aspire to the Pagan priesthood and a commitment to the development of others, the greatest truth held within this virtue is, "If thou wouldst dare to teach, thou must never cease to learn."

## Reincarnation

Reincarnation is a doctrine as well as a virtue. To accept and understand the cycle of birth and death and renewal is to learn to appreciate the constancy of change within the universe, and the ever-present element of hope in each day of life—the promise of life renewed and increased. As Epictitus, the Greek philosopher has said, "As a man, casting off worn out garments taketh new ones, so the dweller in the body, casting off worn out bodies, entereth into ones that are new." The principle of reincarnation embodies and clarifies some of the other traditional Pagan beliefs. The thirst for knowledge and development is explained in the light of the virtue of reincarnation. Know that whatever happens, and to whomever it happens, it is that soul's free will in its efforts to learn and progress. The virtues of reincarnation are capsulated in what Pagans remember as the "Promise of the Cycle, and the Turning of the Wheel." Everything moves in cycles. Every action is karmic. The more one progresses, the closer he or she moves to the Divine realm. The promise is that all will progress. The wheel is not stationary, nor can be the soul. Another Pagan belief embraced by the virtue of reincarnation addresses the eternal fellowship enjoyed by those who follow the old ways. It is believed by many Pagan traditions that we return in the same place and at the same time as those we have loved before—"To meet, to know, to remember, and to love again."

## Harmony

Harmony means to live as one among the cycles of the universe—to see the life that continues within and without us. It is to see ourselves as an integral part of all that exists, and truly know ourselves as the children of divine parentage. Think of all of life as interconnected. Sense all things as part of a divine pattern, woven together in a golden tapestry. To touch one string is to alter the weave. Magick is the manipulation of the woven cloth of the universe.

The responsibility of magick is to know beforehand which golden strand you pull, and how the pattern will be altered.

## Tolerance

Finally, there is the virtue of tolerance. This is an understanding that while each individual must follow his or her own heart, and pursue that which they believe, one person's way is not the right path for all, and is certainly not the only way. Through tolerance we learn patience and serenity. In its purest form, tolerance is not merely "putting up" with the fact that others may approach things differently from what you believe, but it is trying to understand the "whys" behind their ways. Through acceptance of others may also come insights that may have otherwise been undisclosed, since fresh perspectives are often the path to greater understanding.

One of the other traditional pieces that has been used to capture the rites, beliefs, practices and virtues of the Pagan people is known as the Wiccan Rede. There is a short version of this particular piece that is remembered among the people of many traditions today. It heralds the virtues of perfect love and perfect trust, and includes another commonly shared Wiccan/Pagan guide-phrase, "An you harm none, do what you will." However, there is an expanded version of the Wiccan Rede that addresses many more of the Pagan virtues. It was printed in its entirety in the Spring Equinox 1974 edition of the "Earth Religion

News," a Pagan publication that has since stopped printing. In addition to expounding on many of the ritual beliefs and practices of the Old Religion, it addresses virtues of tolerance, fairness, sensitivity, loyalty, and, perhaps most importantly, unity and love among the Pagan people. In fact, every virtue that takes a station upon the wheel can be found in the expanded version of the Wiccan Rede. Unfortunately, this piece was printed without any background information, and no author credit. However, although we cannot identify the source of the piece with any certainty, it has been adopted by several practicing groups who appreciate its value as a Pagan guide to daily and ritual life.

In addition to the Pagan virtues remembered on the wheel, there are many pieces of ritual, many folk tales, rhymes, riddles, and songs that serve the Pagan community as a guide to life. These may be gleaned from the tales and legends of many lands, from the stories passed down by the Irish storytellers, from Gypsy folklore, or even from fairy tales. There are many sources for the ancient wisdom. The marvelous tales that so many of us remember hearing as children may have a message, a moral, that is a reminder of the Pagan virtues, and a remnant of ancient Pagan culture.

Other traditions have ritual bits that are unique to them. Perhaps they are words of wisdom passed down from ages past. Perhaps they are songs from the heart of a newly dedicated Pagan—but the Old

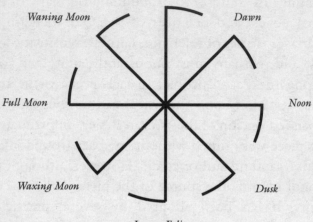

Solar Eclipse

Waning Moon

Dawn

Full Moon

Noon

Waxing Moon

Dusk

Lunar Eclipse

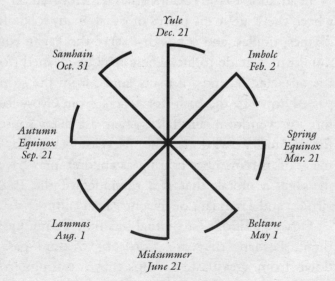

Yule
Dec. 21

Samhain
Oct. 31

Imbolc
Feb. 2

Autumn
Equinox
Sep. 21

Spring
Equinox
Mar. 21

Lammas
Aug. 1

Beltane
May 1

Midsummer
June 21

**Other Pagan Wheels**

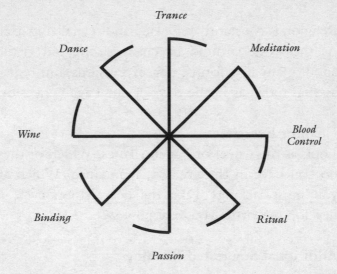

Trance

Dance    Meditation

Wine    Blood
Control

Binding    Ritual

Passion

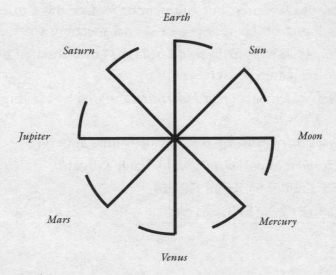

Earth

Saturn    Sun

Jupiter    Moon

Mars    Mercury

Venus

**Other Pagan Wheels**

Religion is constantly renewing and revitalizing itself. As the world around us changes, the old virtues adopt many new forms, new expressions, but remain as vital today as in the days of our Pagan ancestors.

**Chapter Exercises**
Look at the wheel of Pagan virtues. Which of these do you have in the greatest abundance? Which are you most lacking? Take the next Moon cycle to develop the virtue you least possess.

**Additional Suggested Reading**
Because discussion of virtue demands introspection, philosophical material is indicated. Listed here are a few old favorites, but augment or replace these titles with any others that are of special meaning to you.

*The Apology, Phaedo, and Credo of Plato* translated by
    Benjamin Jowlett
*The Golden Sayings of Epictitus* translated by Hastings
    Crossley
*The Little Prince* by Antoine de Saint Exupery
*Thoughts and Meditations* by Kahlil Gibran
*The Prophet* by Kahlil Gibran
*Tao Te Ching* by Lao Tzu

# Chapter Eleven

# *The Priesthood*

The requirements and obligations of the Pagan priesthood may be as varied as the number of different Pagan traditions in evidence today. Because of the need for secrecy to ensure survival in times gone by, there are some Pagan groups that still require initiation into the priesthood before any knowledge of their ways can be passed on. Others prefer that a certain level of knowledge be attained before induction into the priesthood can even be considered. Specific areas of knowledge assigned to each level of priesthood may differ from one practice to another.

Because the variances between one system and the next in regard to the attainment of priesthood can be significant, some of the views offered here are colored by the author's own traditional beliefs and personal experiences. This is presented as one way of approaching the subject of the priesthood, and it should be remembered that it is by no means the only way.

Although there are many groups that still insist on initiation prior to teaching, this is, I think, a trend that is fading. There are probably three main factors that have contributed to this change of heart. First, and most obvious, is that while acceptance of the Pagan people is not complete in modern society, the intensity of the consequences of following one's own heart has lessened—the "burning times" are over. Secondly, it has become apparent to many of the Pagan priesthood that a priesthood with no uninitiated adherents of the Pagan religion is a diluted (and, perhaps, deluded) priesthood. What is the purpose of a priesthood with no gathering of people to whom they can minister? Finally, there is the matter of reason and compassion. If there is a soul who has a Pagan heart, but no aspirations toward priestly duty, should they be denied knowledge and worship of their God and Goddess?

Although there are different approaches to priesthood within different traditions, different levels of training which entitle one to be called a priest or priestess, and different numbers of priesthood degrees, one widely used system is the three level system. These may be called first, second, and third degree, maiden, mother, crone, young lord, father, sage, neophyte, priest/priestess, high priest/high priestess, or any number of other chosen titles. Within my own tradition, we simply call these levels of responsibility and training the first rite, the second rite, and the third rite. The guidelines that follow have been taken from my own tradition, and may be unfamiliar to some. However, having seen similar systems in place in different traditions throughout North America, I can say that this is one approach that is widely used, and worthy of note.

The first level of priesthood is a time of preparation, a time to work on internal development. The priesthood is responsible for the welfare of the Pagan people. The initial task at hand upon joining the ranks of the Pagan priesthood is to develop one's own virtue to such an extent to be worthy of the great responsibility of the welfare of others.

In this time, knowledge and training may be concentrated in the areas of Pagan history, mythology, meditation, basic precepts of magick, sabbat and esbat rituals and legends, reincarnation, and understanding the rites of passage. It is a time to work on discipline and self-control. This is the beginning of work on becoming master of one's emotions and developing poise under stress. It is a time to begin simplifying one's life.

Often, the first degree priest or priestess is given a great deal of advice and guidance by their initiators. At this point, it is self-development that is most highly emphasized. The new initiate is given as much guidance and support as is needed. The sincere initiate is self-aware, is willing to work as hard as is necessary to fulfill the degree, is honest about his or her knowledge or position, and is as keenly aware of how much there is to learn.

Upon elevation to second degree, responsibilities increase as the priest or priestess begins to apply the teachings, and, in some traditions, begins teaching others. Training does not stop, however. It may be expanded to include divination and tarot, scrying, runes, developing clairvoyance within oneself as well as in others, herbal lore, massage, and techniques of psychic healing.

Attention is turned to the practice of charity, devotion, patience, kindness, sincerity, courage, precision, efficiency, and discernment. This is often the time when a hundred obstacles and doubts take hold of the developing priest or priestess, and a hundred trials follow close at their heels. As the devoted priest or priestess passes through these obstacles, the mind expands and changes, and the virtue strengthens. This is when it hits home that, at any level of the priesthood, one is an example and a role model to those to whom you minister, those who you teach. The ever-present obligation to act accordingly may, at times, weigh heavy.

At the third level of priesthood, one is dedicated formally and completely to the Pagan way. This dedication arises from within, and may truly be felt at any degree level. The third rite is but an outward sign of the sealing. True initiation is at the hands of the God and Goddess. At this point, one should have mastered the rites and rituals, and should have a good general knowledge in a wide variety of areas of study. Many decide to specialize at this point.

In many traditions, the third degree is "on call" for whenever a need arises. This is the level at which one becomes known as a High Priest or High Priestess, whose life belongs to the service of the Deities and the Pagan people. This service is a privilege and honor.

The quest for higher levels of knowledge continues at this point, when knowledge is at its greatest point of development—but the single greatest insight is often the realization of how much remains to be learned. Improvement of the personality is still of paramount importance as one strives to know and to do the will of the Deities.

This is a time when we turn to linking our energies and character to the God and Goddess. We work hard for the benefit of the Pagan people and humanity in general, and continue to improve and increase our knowledge and understanding.

There is yet another phase of the priesthood that is given honor among a great many Pagan groups, though it may be viewed in different manners. This is the office of Elder. In some groups, a Priest or Priestess is considered an Elder at the point in which they begin teaching others. Some traditions consider anyone who has been elevated to second degree or higher to be an Elder. Others hold a single office of Elder within their traditions. In this case, the Elder is the highest ranking of the priesthood, often considered the Father or Mother of the group. As the high priesthood is available twenty-four hours a day to the Pagan community, so is the Elder available, not only to the Pagan people, but to the priesthood as well.

The Elder must have a sound knowledge of other traditions as well as his or her own, including a solid working knowledge of ritual and magick. In some traditions, the office of Elder is largely one of honor. In others, it is one of intense responsibility, not only within the particular tradition, but as a representative of the tradition within the Pagan community at large.

As already stated, this is but one approach to the Pagan priesthood. There are some traditions that have as many as nine, twelve, or thirteen different levels of initiation. There are some that have only one. Some may not consider an initiate at all levels to be a member of the priesthood, while others do. There are differences in the required training and level of development at each level between varying traditions. Some traditions accept self-initiation, while others do not.

But all of these variances are of little more than academic concern. Each practice comes with its own systems, its own constraints. That is what makes one tradition different from another, and what makes one practice comfortable for one, yet ill-suited to another. And it is in these differences that the lessons of unity, tolerance, and respect are learned.

For many, there is no great aspiration to serve as a Priest or Priestess. Some might prefer to till the earth, raise a temple to their honor, or write a song of adoration. Some may simply be of Pagan heart, but have no inclination to the priesthood. For these people, many groups have developed groves that enable them to participate in rituals, and follow the Old Religion without the mandate of joining the priesthood. For those who wish to formalize their commitment to Paganism without initiation into the priesthood, many traditions offer dedication rites, so that they may proclaim their adoration of the Old Ones and affirm their commitment to a Pagan way of life yet not obligate themselves to becoming a Priest or Priestess of the religion. Then again, there is always the path of solitary practice. One need not become an initiated member of the priesthood to adore the God and Goddess in lone ritual. Certainly, they would care more about the sincerity of one's heart than the trappings of a particular tradition.

Whatever the differences between different practices, the office of the priesthood is not without responsibility, and should not be taken lightly. In the deepest sense, the Priest or Priestess is an instrument of the Divine, through whom the Pagan people may give honor to the God and Goddess. The priesthood exists in service to the Deities and to the Pagan people—this is the essence of its purpose.

**Chapter Exercises**
Consider if you have any aspirations to become initiated into the Pagan priesthood. Do some soul searching. How much are you willing to study? How much of yourself are you willing to dedicate to others who seek the old ways?

If you have no desire to become a priest or priestess, or if it is a goal for further off in the future, what can you do to honor the God and Goddess, to nourish the Earth and the gifts of nature? Are you willing?

**Additional Suggested Reading**
Whether you have discovered a definite affinity toward becoming one of the priesthood, have decided that it may not be the path for you, or simply have not made a definite determination, it may be a good time to read the personal stories of another who has made the commitment. Try these titles:

*Diary of a Witch* by Sybil Leek

*The Art of Witchcraft* by Sybil Leek

# Chapter Twelve

## *Paganism as a Way of Life*

There are some modern-day Pagans who find some degree of conflict in living their lives in accordance with the old ways, and, in fact, there may be a need for reinterpretation of some

Pagan customs and traditions in order to fit with today's social structure. Essentially, the root of Pagan worship is the attunement with the natural order of the universe, the celebration of natural cycles, and a reverence for the Deities of nature and all that they have given.

Historically, the Pagan people have been those who lived close to the land, such as the farmers, hunters, and fishermen. It was they who could most readily observe and appreciate the wonders of the natural order. When a farmer watched a sprout appear through the brown soil, or a fisherman steered his vessel by the faithful guidance of the North Star, or a hunter prayed to the Horned God for the success of the hunt, the power and benevolence of nature was evident.

Today, however, the life within nature has become less apparent to many, as men and women work within the "social order" as opposed to the natural world. Today, many Pagan people are accountants, psychologists, inventory clerks, sales people, hair stylists, dancers, or factory workers. Unlike their ancestors, who were not only close to nature but dependent on it, they live and work largely removed from the natural world. How can the modern Pagan learn to appreciate what has been torn from daily existence by time and "progress"? In a world of steel and concrete, how can one appreciate the wildflowers and beasts of the untamed lands?

It should be remembered that it is not nature that has hidden from humanity, but humanity that has attempted to overshadow nature with the artifices of its own existence. The Sun and Moon rise as brightly above the high-rise as they do above the mountain lake. The green sprout in the flower box is rich with the same force of life that helped the ancient oak grow to its grand stature.

We have created a world of our own making, often raping nature in the process. Witness the polluted rivers that cry out for a return to the days of clean water and healthy fish, or how the air, robbed of its clear freshness, now threatens its polluters in turn.

In some ways, it may be argued that the urban Pagan is no further from the natural world than those few who still make their living tilling the land. Where the city-bound Pagan seldom sees the fields as they mature from first planting to the ripeness of the harvest, the modern farmer has largely lost touch with nature's life and power. It is not as easy to see and to feel and to appreciate the life and growth of the wheat as it may have been in times past. The hand of our ancestors could feel the life of the ear of corn they plucked from the stalk at harvest time—the blades of the thresher are not quite so sensitive to all that went into the creation of this ripened life. Does the milking machine appreciate the gift of the cow, or the cotton gin appreciate that the fields yield their crop? Do any of the modern agricultural machines recognize their close ties to the gifts of the God and Goddess? How far removed from the earth are the operators of this modern equipment?

It is within this apparent absence of the natural order that the devout Pagan might see nature most clearly, and do the greatest honor to the Pagan God and Goddess. Like a child who has lost a favored trinket, the value of the toy is most clearly evident in its absence. So are the gifts of nature most appreciated in their loss. And those who expend their efforts in the work of restoring the natural order live every day to the honor of the Deities.

One of the purposes of the Pagan bond to nature is learning. Through reflection on the cycles of nature, one may gain insight into the world in which we live, as well as an understanding of one's fellows and of the inner workings of one's being. This is as valid today as it was when Pagans worked and lived in close connection to the earth. The main difference today may be where we look to find the natural order.

It is wonderful, every now and then, to retreat to the woods and see the lands in their untainted glory. It is an act of worship to renew the old bonds to the earth, and to the Deities that make themselves apparent in every bud of every flower, every ripple in the flowing waters. Yet the essence of a Pagan lifestyle is to see the thread of nature that runs throughout all of life. The spirits of the elements can be found in all places. There have been as many who have befriended the gnomes in their own gardens as in the open fields. The salamanders, spirits of fire, are as at home in the hearth fire as in the balefire lit in the outdoor circle. Sylphs have been encountered in the blue chlorinated water of the swimming pool as well as playing upon the crests of the ocean waves. The winds that carry fairies here and there blow through city parks as well as country orchards. Despite the efforts of technology, nature is still very much with us. It is there for the sincere Pagan who has the eyes to see it.

Look even at the domesticated animals we keep in our home for companionship. Watch the reaction of birds just prior to a storm. See how they herald the coming tempest. Note that your dog is there to meet you at the front door before you have a chance to turn the doorknob. Do a ritual in the presence of your cat. Does the feline instinct not recognize the spirits of nature as you welcome them?

Whether you make your home in the bosom of the forest, in a houseboat on the river, in the heart of the wild jungle, amid the domesticated greenery of suburbia, or in an apartment in the largest of cities, nature is all around you. Nature is alive in every living thing. It is apparent in the innate wisdom called instinct retained by even domesticated beasts. It is evident in the bonding of man and woman as one, in birth, in death, and in the constancy of change. And the God and Goddess themselves are apparent within every fiber of their creations.

To live as a Pagan is simply to understand and appreciate the Pagan virtues, to see and appreciate the gifts of nature, and to honor the God and Goddess through everything you do. It is said in an old morsel of wisdom carried in the handwritten books of my own tradition, and, perhaps, still remembered by some of the country folk:

> "An' ye be loyal and loving to each living thing, ye be giving honor most high to those who did create them."

**Chapter Exercises**
Begin to keep a daily journal: not a record of events of what transpired each day, but a log of what you've learned each day from keeping your eyes and ears and heart open to the natural world around you. Keep it for as long as you like.(This was first suggested to me about twenty-two years ago, and to this day I still may be found noting the lessons that become apparent in everyday life.)

**Additional Suggested Reading**
*The Family Wicca Book* by Ashleen O'Gaea
*The Urban Pagan: Magickal Living in a 9–5 World* by Patricia Telesco

# Chapter Thirteen

# *Conclusion*

There are so many areas of study connected with a Pagan lifestyle. In exploring and embracing the ways of the craeft, there may be some learning in the fields of natural sciences such as herbalism, aromatherapy, and healing massage. Personal development may be pursued through the practice of the divinatory arts like astrology, the Tarot, scrying, runes, or palmistry. Natural Magick may be the path chosen to find one's place within the universe and learn how the universe of the God and Goddess all fits together.

What has been offered here is a basic overview. Hopefully, it will be enough for the seeker to determine whether the Pagan way is the chosen path for further study, and enough to open up the potentials of other traditions to practicing Pagans. It should be remembered, however, that this offering is intended only as an overview, a very general look at what Paganism is all about.

The bits and pieces contained in *Pagan Ways* are designed to give a solid foundation with which to take a first step. It is an indication of what practicing Pagans see in the path they follow, and a hint at the benefits they enjoy in their daily and ritual observances. It also contains some pieces of actual Pagan practice that will serve as a taste of reality to the new seeker of the old path, and a glimpse of some alternative ways of thought to the practicing Pagan.

Much of what has been contained in this work has been gathered from the notes from my own introductory Pagan teachings. These bits of information have served well as a basis for teaching, and have served those well who have continued in a Pagan way of life. Some students have continued on to become dedicated Pagans, or initiated Priests and Priestesses. Others have chosen other paths. As much an endorsement of this particular introductory presentation as the practicing Pagans that have taken their first steps with these studies are those who have chosen alternate paths because there was another road that may have been more suited to them at the time. This is a choice that could not have been wisely made without knowing what Paganism actually is.

It is the responsibility of the Pagan Priesthood to guide and to educate in the ways of the Deities. Whether through books, lectures, or other communication media, whether through personal teaching, or a passing shared insight, each soul that has been helped along the path of his or her own development is a credit to the work of the God and Goddess. Those who truly are of Pagan mind and heart, upon reading this volume, may gain a sense of security and well-being in knowing that their feet are turned in the right direction. They need only fine-tune their decision by choosing a tradition that seems to best reflect their own beliefs and preferences.

Those who realize that their direction lies elsewhere will be equally benefited by their study of *Pagan Ways* as they learn that their hearts lie upon another path. Either way, as each seeker learns the direction that is right for him or her, it is to the greater glory of the Deities that they have been guided along their road to personal development and fulfillment.

Whereas much of the published work on Paganism is directed toward the would-be Pagan or wanna-be Witch, *Pagan Ways* is written for those who wish to learn about the old ways. It is designed as an enabler, to help in offering enough understanding and insight to allow a fully thought-out and firm decision as to whether or not this is, indeed, the path for the individual reader.

Choose to embrace the ways of the old religion, and honor the Pagan God and Goddess—or not, as the heart demands. Either way, may the blessings of all that the Pagan world has to offer, the heart of every Pagan practitioner, and the favor of the Deities be always at your side.

## Chapter Exercise

If you have enjoyed your venture into the Pagan world, reflect upon it and gain what you might. If it is a world that seems unsuited to you, then go onward to the path that will be more fulfilling, and know that this is but one path of many to take on a spiritual journey. And if it seems right to you, if you find you are of a Pagan heart, then light a candle to the honor of the God and Goddess, and begin to live the life that you were meant to live.

## Additional Suggested Reading

*Maiden, Mother, Crone: The Myth and Reality of the Triple Goddess* by D. J. Conway

*Witchcraft from the Inside* by Raymond Buckland

# Afterword

Over twenty years ago, when the author first began to teach Paganism through ritual and one-on-one teaching arrangements, the number of Pagans and would-be Pagans was far more limited than they are today. It was far easier to disseminate information about the Old Religion in a personal and sensitive way. Since then, however, the Pagan world has increased many times in size.

The religion itself has undergone changes of significant proportions. Where Paganism was once comprised of a handful of traditions that survived along with a handful of newly created practices developed through dedicated research of times past, the different expressions of Pagan practice today are almost limitless.

Some of the changes we have seen have not necessarily been positive for the rediscovery of Pagan ways. Because traditions were closely held, they were often under the direction of one or two individuals and subject to the human frailties of their chief administrators. In extreme cases, seekers might find themselves involved in a group in which they are following an individual, rather than finding their way to the God and Goddess.

Perhaps as a rebellion against this kind of circumstance, more and more Pagans chose to worship in private, away from the demands of individuals and organizations. While an act of sincerity and honor in one sense, this path is not without its own inherent problems. In losing touch with groups and individuals who form and control Pagan covens and alliances, many have also cut themselves off from the depth of the knowledge that these groups and individuals have to offer. The resulting solitary practice is often a hit-or-miss kind of proposition.

Yet, years ago, when the Pagan world was smaller, there were certain criteria that seemed a common yardstick by which to measure the sincerity of most practices, regardless of the particular tradition they observed. These common points seem to have become obscured, and are not widely taught today. But they remain as valid as they have always been.

It is in the rediscovery of this common ground that lies the importance of *Pagan Ways*. This book is written as a Pagan overview. Within its pages are heralded those things that make the Pagan people one people, though they may practice their beliefs in many different ways. It is an offering of the values that priests and priestesses of different traditions held universally, though their ways might differ markedly in other respects.

*Pagan Ways* is also a statement of sorts. One of the shared principles of groups that were in evidence twenty years ago is that you may sell your own arts, your own abilities, your own efforts—but that which is of the God and Goddess is NOT FOR SALE. Certainly, if you offer an herbal remedy or read the Tarot for someone, there is no reason that the cost of the herbs should come out of your own pocket, nor your efforts in reading go unrewarded. However, in teaching Paganism, the way of the Deities, it is not for a mortal to place a price tag on the value.

Paganism has always been a religion of the common people, not of the rich and powerful. It cannot be bought and sold. Yet, today, there are many who charge dearly for classes in the Old Religion. Yes, an individual's time and effort are worth something, and a nominal charge is not out of order. But to charge for the knowledge itself or for the promise of initiation into the priesthood is to cheapen the quality of the gift. The only true dedication and initiation is in the hands of the God and Goddess, and no individual can in good conscience charge a fee for that which the Deities offer freely.

In offering *Pagan Ways*, it is hoped that we are taking a step toward a rediscovery of the Old

Religion—but also a rediscovery of the values of honor that were once a part of Pagan practice and of the Pagan people.

# Glossary

**Air.** One of the four basic elements. Air is often associated with dawn and the East in ritual practice.

**Alexandrian.** A Pagan tradition developed by and resulting from the research and training of Alex Sanders. This has become a far-reaching tradition with groups throughout the world.

**Athame.** A black-handled ritual knife used in ceremony to direct energies.

**Beltane.** One of the traditional Pagan festivals, celebrated on May eve.

**Book of Shadows.** Ritual book used in Pagan rites.

**Candlemas.** Pagan celebration observed on February 2.

**Circle.** A space consecrated for use in Pagan worship; also a common name for ritual work itself.

**Coven.** A group of practicing Pagans. It traditionally numbers thirteen in membership, but may have any small number of members.

**Craeft.** An often-used name for the old religion, probably originating from an archaic spelling of the word *witchcraft*. Also know as the "Craeft of the Wise" (see Wicca).

**Dedication.** A ritual of commitment to the study and practice of Paganism. A vow of allegiance to the old ways and to the Gods and Goddesses. In some traditions, this rite is known as "Paganing."

**Earth.** One of the four basic elements. This element is often, though not always, associated with midnight and the North.

**Elder.** An office of authority among many Pagan traditions. There are varying responsibilities connected with this title and different criteria by which it is earned, depending on the particular group.

**Fairies.** A general classification for elemental spirits of the air.

**Fire.** One of the four key elements of Pagan belief, often associated with noon and the South.

**Gardnerian.** The tradition that has grown from the work of Dr. Gerald Gardner. Dating back to the 1950s, it is one of the first publicly acknowledged reformulations of the craeft. Many other traditions take their format from Gardnerian practice.

**Gnomes.** Earth elementals.

**God.** The male deity of the Pagans, also known as Lord of the Hunt, All Father, or by any of the male God names that survive in varying mythologies (i.e., Pan, Odin, Mithras, Cerrunnos, etc.).

**Goddess.** The female principal of Pagan worship, also remembered as the Great Mother, the Lady, or mythological Goddess names such as Diana, Artemis, Hecate, Danu, etc.

**Hereditary.** Pagan practitioner of a tradition that has been carried on through the family along successive generations. Because of the nature of the family traditions, and the obligation to continue the line of practice through their own families, they often keep their traditions largely to themselves and often practice their ways privately, although they may interact with other groups.

**High Priest/Priestess.** An initiated priest of the Pagan people. Often the third level of priesthood, although it may vary according to tradition.

**Initiation.** The ritual that binds an individual to the old religion. It may also qualify him or her as a Priest or Priestess and religious leader of the Pagan people, depending on tradition. Initiation is on three different levels in some traditions, reflecting the degree of training and the level of responsibility. However, other practices may have systems with more or less distinct levels.

**Karma.** A universal law adhered to by most practicing Pagans, stating that the good that people do will return to them, as well as the evil. Karma creates circumstances through which we learn about consequence and widen our perspective to include the viewpoints of others.

**Magick.** The ability and knowledge to work with and manipulate the forces of nature. There are basically two different kinds of magickal practice. The first is an extension of will and arises from within. The second utilizes forces from outside the practicing magician—elemental spirits, deities, angels, etc. The forces used may be determined by the particular belief system of the practitioner.

**Old Religion.** Another name for Paganism in its many forms. The term arises because the roots of Paganism may be found in the furthest reaches of history, and even prehistory.

**Pagan.** A follower of the Old Religion of the Gods and Goddesses of Nature. This derives from the root word *pagani*, meaning the people of the fields. It is a good descriptive root for those who are tied to the land and revere Nature.

**Pentagram.** A five-sided star within a circle. A favored symbol among many Pagan groups, it symbolizes Humanity in form and essence. It also represents the four elements of earth, air, fire, and water and that which ties them together: spirit. The pentagram has a multiplicity of meanings, but is widely used as a Pagan symbol.

**Promise of the Cycle/Turning of the Wheel.** This is a widely held doctrine of the Old Religion which refers to the constant march of change, the promise of progress and development, and the gift of rebirth and renewal (as in reincarnation).

**Reincarnation.** A belief, held by Pagans and some others, that each soul is reborn into successive lives as it learns and progresses.

**Rites of Passage.** Ritual observances that mark transitionary periods in one's life such as birth, death, marriage, initiation, and dedication.

**Rune.** A symbolic figure with specific meaning, often used in cryptic communication as well as magick.

**Sabbat.** Any of the major seasonal festivals of the Pagan people, timed by the position of the Sun.

**Samhain.** The Feast of the Dead or World's Meet, which is celebrated on November eve.

**Salamanders.** Elemental spirits of fire.

**Solitary.** A practitioner of the Old Religion who worships privately, outside of a group or coven.

**Sylphs.** Elemental spirits of water.

**Traditionalists.** Pagan practitioners who adopt the customs, mythologies, culture, and language of a specific country or people within their ritual and practice of the Old Religion.

**Water.** The element generally associated with sunset and the Western realm.

**Wicca.** A relatively new phrase (arising within the last thirty years) to describe Pagan practitioners. It comes from the Anglo Saxon root word *wicce*, meaning to know. Hence, many modern Pagans, in their quest for continued knowledge, consider themselves engaged in the '"Craeft of the Wise."

**Witch.** As regards Pagan religion, a witch is simply a Pagan priest or priestess. However, because the connotations that have built up over the centuries tend to overshadow the actual meaning with visions of something that is evil, or spooky, or eerie, many members of the priesthood tend to avoid the term.

# Additional Reading

Although there are many quality volumes available on Paganism and Wicca, certain books stand in the forefront as especially valuable for research and continued learning. I like to think of these as "Gwydion's Bibles."

**General Reading**

Buckland, Raymond. *Complete Book of Witchcraft*. St Paul, MN: Llewellyn Publications, 1986.

**Background and History**

Valiente, Doreen. *An ABC of Witchcraft*. Custer, WA: Phoenix Publishing, Inc., 1984.

**Mythology**

Guest, Lady Charlotte. *The Mabinogion*. Chicago, IL: Academy Chi Pubs, 1978.

Frazer, Sir James George. *The Golden Bough*. New York: Macmillan Publishing Company, Inc., 1985.

Graves, Robert. *The White Goddess*. Magnolia, MA: Peter Smith Publishing, Inc., 1983.

O'Hara, Gwydion. *Sun Lore: Myths and Folklore From Around the World*. St, Paul, MN: Llewellyn Publications, 1997.

Conway, D. J. *Ancient and Shining Ones: World Myth, Magick, and Religion*. St Paul, MN: Llewellyn Publications, 1994. (An invaluable reference work! This is already listed in the text, but could stand another mention. It is an asset to any Pagan library.)

Also, any of the widely available works on mythology of any kind (J. Campbell is tops in the field).

## Traditions

Farrar, Janet and Stewart. *The Witches' Way*. New York: State Mutual Book, 1988.

Martello, Leo Louis. *Witchcraft, the Old Religion*. New York: Carol Publishing Group, 1987.

# ☾ LOOK FOR THE CRESCENT MOON

*Llewellyn publishes hundreds of books on your favorite subjects! To get these exciting books, including the ones on the following pages, check your local bookstore or order them directly from Llewellyn.*

## ORDER BY PHONE
- Call toll-free within the U.S. and Canada, 1-800-THE MOON
- In Minnesota, call (612) 291-1970
- We accept VISA, MasterCard, and American Express

## ORDER BY MAIL
- Send the full price of your order (MN residents add 7% sales tax) in U.S. funds, plus postage & handling to:

    Llewellyn Worldwide
    P.O. Box 64383, Dept. K341-7
    St. Paul, MN 55164–0383, U.S.A.

## POSTAGE & HANDLING
(For the U.S., Canada, and Mexico)
- $4.00 for orders $15.00 and under
- $5.00 for orders over $15.00
- No charge for orders over $100.00

We ship UPS in the continental United States. We ship standard mail to P.O. boxes. Orders shipped to Alaska, Hawaii, The Virgin Islands, and Puerto Rico are sent first-class mail. Orders shipped to Canada and Mexico are sent surface mail.

**International orders:** Airmail—add freight equal to price of each book to the total price of order, plus $5.00 for each non-book item (audio tapes, etc.).

**Surface mail**—Add $1.00 per item.

*Allow 4–6 weeks for delivery on all orders.*
*Postage and handling rates subject to change.*

## DISCOUNTS
We offer a 20% discount to group leaders or agents. You must order a minimum of 5 copies of the same book to get our special quantity price.

## FREE CATALOG
Get a free copy of our color catalog, *New Worlds of Mind and Spirit*. Subscribe for just $10.00 in the United States and Canada ($30.00 overseas, airmail). Many bookstores carry *New Worlds*—ask for it!

**Visit our web site at www.llewellyn.com for more information.**

## Moon Lore:
## Myths & Folklore from Around the World
### Gwydion O'Hara

Most of us love stories. But the rich messages spun in folklore—especially in oral traditions—are not found in the media from which we get most of our knowledge today. Fairy tales rehashed in media mega-productions don't often serve the true function of a fairy or folk tale. Where are the stories that entertain, enlighten, and bring us closer together?

*Moon Lore* is a collection of tales about the people of many lands and times. The common thread connecting the stories is the Moon: the heavenly body that has guided us since the beginning of time. Today, Moon mythology continues to bind the people of the world together, reflecting our diverse lives in all her faces. *Moon Lore*'s magical characters and settings spring to life in tales of jealousy, fear, triumph, celebration, love, and challenge. Find out what the Hindi Wise men see in the Moon (it's not a man's face). Jack and Jill are in *Moon Lore*, but in this Germanic variation, magic brew is what they fetch, and they never tumble down the hill! Chapters are divided into 13 segments, each lunar month presenting a new myth from Celtic, Chinese, Native American, and other traditions and cultures.

1-56718-342-5
256 pp., 5 ¼ x 8, index, softcover                    $12.95

## Sun Lore:
## Myths & Folklore from
## Around the World
### Gwydion O'Hara

Tales of simplicity and glory ... death and life ... compassion and devastation—there is little that has not been within the reaches of the Sun. From the beginning of time, when getting through each new day was an end in itself, the sun watched overhead.

*Sun Lore* is a bridge between the primitive man who lived and worshiped according to those things that were beyond understanding, and the modern man of reason who attempts to analyze the world in which we live. These illustrated tales are a celebration of the Sun worshipers of ancient times, offered up for the insight and enjoyment of their descendants who dwell in an age of science.

Read stories from around the world about the creation of life, about how each Sun God and Goddess came to be, and folk tales about the Sun as hero and fool. In experiencing the old legends of Father Sun, we can realign ourselves with the forgotten times that hold the roots of our modern existence and shape our families, faith, and cultures.

1-56718-343-3
224 pp., 5 ¼ x 8, illus., softcover                    $9.95

**To order, call 1-800-THE MOON**
Prices subject to change without notice

## Inside a Witches' Coven
### Edain McCoy

*Inside a Witches' Coven* gives you an insider's look at how a real Witches' coven operates, from initiation and secret vows to parting rituals. You'll get step-by-step guidance for joining or forming a coven, plus sage advice and exclusive insights to help you decide which group is the right one for you.

Maybe you're thinking about joining a coven, but don't know what to expect, or how to make contacts. Perhaps you already belong to a coven, but your group needs ideas for organizing a teaching circle or mediating conflicts. Either way, you're sure to find *Inside a Witches' Coven* a practical source of wisdom.

Joining a coven can be an important step in your spiritual life. Before you take that step, let a practicing Witch lead you through the hidden inner workings of a Witches' coven.

1-56718-666-1
224 pp., 5 ¼ x 8, softcover                                    $9.95

**To order, call 1-800-THE MOON**
Prices subject to change without notice

**Lord of Light & Shadow:**
The Many Faces of the God
D. J. Conway

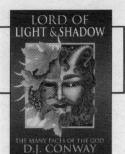

Early humans revered the great Goddess and all Her personalized aspects, but they also revered the God as Her necessary and important consort/lover/son. *Lord of Light and Shadow* leads you through the myths of the world's diverse cultures to find the archetypal Pagan God hidden behind all of them. He is a being with the traits and aspects that women secretly desire in men, and that men desire to emulate. The patriarchal religions assimilated the ancient spirit of the Pagan God—in one form or another—into their scriptures. Yet, despite the deliberate changes to his identity, there is something about the God that could never be destroyed. By searching for the original Pagan God in these mythologies, you will find his spiritual essence and the path to the truth.

1-56178-177-5
240 pp., 6 x 9, illus., softcover                    $14.95

## The Wiccan Mysteries:
### Ancient Origins & Teachings
### Raven Grimassi

What you will encounter in *The Wiccan Mysteries* is material that was once taught only in the initiate levels of the old Wiccan Mystery Traditions, and to which many solitary practitioners have never had access. Learn the inner meanings of Wiccan rites, beliefs and practices, and discover the time-proven concepts that created, maintained and carried Wiccan beliefs up into this modern era. In reflecting back upon the wisdom of our ancestors, neo-Wiccans can draw even greater sustenance from the spiritual stores of Wicca—the Old Religion.

*The Wiccan Mysteries* will challenge you to expand your understanding and even re-examine your own perceptions. Wicca is essentially a Celtic-oriented religion, but its Mystery Tradition is derived from several outside cultures as well. You will come away with a sense of the rich heritage that was passed from one human community to another, and that now resides within this system for spiritual development.

1-56718-254-2
312 pp., 6 x 9, softcover                                        $14.95

**To order, call 1-800-THE MOON**
Prices subject to change without notice

# Glamoury:
## Magic of the Celtic Green World
### Steve Blamires

Glamoury refers to an Irish Celtic magical tradition that is truly holistic, satisfying the needs of the practitioner on the physical, mental, and spiritual levels. This guidebook offers practical exercises and modern versions of time-honored philosophies that will expand your potential into areas previously closed to you.

We have moved so far away from our ancestors' closeness to the Earth—the Green World—that we have nearly forgotten some very important truths about human nature. *Glamoury* brings these truths to light so you can take your rightful place in the Green World. Experience the world in a more balanced, meaningful way. Meet helpers and guides from the Otherworld who will become your valued friends. Live in tune with the seasons and gauge your inner growth in relation to the Green World around you.

The ancient Celts couched their wisdom in stories and legends. Today, intuitive people can learn much from these tales. *Glamoury* presents a system based on Irish Celtic mythology to guide you back to the harmony with life's cycles that our ancestors knew.

1-56718-069-8
352 pp., 6 x 9, illus., softcover                    $16.95

## Celtic Myth & Magick: Harnessing the Power of the Gods and Goddesses
### Edain McCoy

Tap into the mythic power of the Celtic goddesses, gods, heroes and heroines to aid your spiritual quests and magickal goals. *Celtic Myth & Magick* explains how to use creative ritual and pathworking to align yourself with the energy of these archetypes, whose potent images live deep within your psyche.

*Celtic Myth & Magick* begins with an overview of 49 different types of Celtic Paganism followed today, then gives specific instructions for evoking and invoking the energy of the Celtic pantheon. Three detailed pathworking texts will take you on an inner journey where you'll join forces with the archetypal images of Cuchulain, Queen Maeve and Merlin the Magician to bring their energies directly into your life. The last half of the book clearly details the energies of over 300 Celtic deities and mythic figures so you can evoke or invoke the appropriate deity to attain a specific goal.

This inspiring, well-researched book will help solitary Pagans who seek to expand the boundaries of their practice to form working partnerships with the divine.

1–56718–661–0
464 pp., 7 x 10, softcover                                    $19.95

**To order, call 1-800-THE MOON**
Prices subject to change without notice